The
Church
and the
Dechurched

The
Church
and the
Dechurched
Mending a Damaged Faith

Mary Tuomi Hammond

Chalice Press®
St. Louis, Missouri

Bible quotations, unless otherwise noted, are taken from the *Today's English Version—Second Edition* © 1992 by American Bible Society. Used by Permission.

Quotations marked NRSV are from the *New Revised Standard Version Bible,* copyright 1989, Division of Christian Education of the National Council of the Churches of Christ in the United States of America. Used by permission. All rights reserved.

Quotations marked KJV are from the *King James Version of the Bible.*

Words from the song "What Am I Doing Here?" quoted on p. 7 are used by permission, Kenneth P. Medema, January 9, 1991, PA 516-802.

Cover design: Dwane Carter
Interior design: Elizabeth Wright
Art direction: Michael Domínguez

This book is printed on acid-free, recycled paper.

Visit Chalice Press on the World Wide Web at
www.chalicepress.com

10 9 8 7 6 5 4 3 2 1   01 02 03 04 05 06

Library of Congress Cataloging–in–Publication Data

Hammond, Mary Tuomi.
     The church and the dechurched : mending a damaged faith / Mary Tuomi
Hammond.
          p.   cm.
     Includes bibliographical references and index.
     ISBN 0-8272-0486-8 (pbk. : alk. paper)
     1. Church attendance. I. Title.
     BV652.5 .H36   2001
     269'.2—dc21   2001000895

Printed in the United States of America

Contents

Acknowledgments

Several people have been an enormous help to me in completing this book, making it possible to share this material with others. My wonderful husband of twenty-six years and partner in ministry, Steve, believed in this project continually, even when my own confidence lagged. The late Sandie Heizer, my beloved area minister for thirteen years, provided a constant source of support for the unique ministry that God has given my husband and me to do, even when it often remained misunderstood by others.

Church member Yvonne Garland and former church member Peter Ossulston, Oberlin College Class of '80, committed themselves to faithful prayer for the manuscript to reach the stage of publication. Their words of encouragement along the way have meant a lot to me. Mary Mild, staff member in the National Offices of the American Baptist Churches, shared her editorial expertise by reviewing the manuscript and providing invaluable suggestions during the writing process. My friend Betsy Ames trusted me with her own story of alienation from the church while offering me the incredible gift of her support and encouragement for this project. Betsy's enthusiasm reminded me again and again of the people I most yearn to touch, whose journeys are near and dear to my heart and to the heart of God.

I want to offer my deepest thanks to my editor at Chalice Press, David Polk, for his encouragement, advice, and support for this project. I also want to thank the Chalice Press publishing house, which has demonstrated its courage and commitment by tackling some of the toughest issues the church must face in this day and time.

I need to thank those individuals who were willing to take the time and energy to fill out the surveys of the dechurched, which form an important section of the book. Many whom I asked declined, not desiring to delve so deeply into their past wounds and struggles with the church. I invite readers to fill out the Dechurched Survey found in chapter 18 as well, if they feel so moved. Since the writing of this book, The First Baptist Church of Oberlin has changed its name to Peace Community Church.

Stories and testimonies can be sent to the author at Peace Community Church, 44 E. Lorain St., Oberlin, OH 44074. Readers may also log on to the church's website at http://www.peacecommunity.mychurch.com.

Copastoring the congregation of The First Baptist Church of Oberlin/Peace Community Church with my husband has been one of the great joys of my life. The dechurched folk who hesitantly made their way into the life of the church over the years have helped me articulate a vision for the church that is continually renewed by their presence. The congregation has rejoiced with me, struggled alongside me, and held me up through the long process of birthing this book.

Finally, I need to express my appreciation to all the dechurched people throughout my life who have shared their pain, alienation, and hope with me. Without their stories, this book would not exist. I have learned so much from each and every life. As humans, we are blessed in the most unsuspecting ways. I am forever indebted to the dechurched for the ways God has worked in my life through them.

Introduction

I heard the word *dechurched* in a conversation several years ago, and it stuck with me. It is a word that cannot be found in either Webster's unabridged dictionary or a pastor's Bible dictionary. It is not a term of common usage in the mainstream church. I use the word *dechurched* as a limited, yet helpful, description for those who have left the church and/or their Christian faith.

Rabid atheists, silent agnostics, and committed humanists are found among this population. Others embrace spiritualities far removed from the basic tenets of Christianity. Some have left communities of faith yet remain believers. All of these people are dechurched.

A large part of my twenty years in ministry has been devoted to working among the dechurched and formerly dechurched. Many of these individuals have been negatively affected by encounters with professing Christians. Their histories in the church are varied, yet often bear the common thread of disillusionment. Pain and alienation become their shared experience.

The word *dechurched* is hardly adequate in describing the variety of individuals in question. Any term that utilizes "church" as its root can easily be misunderstood due to the myriad of popular conceptions and definitions applied to it. Does the word *dechurched* include those who simply neglect to make time for public worship or those who drift away from Christianity out of disinterest and distraction? Does the term primarily refer to individuals who have left mainstream denominations due to serious concerns? Can one be considered dechurched by virtue of simply attending a church and leaving it, regardless of whether that person ever made a genuine commitment to a life of Christian discipleship?

With these very valid questions in mind, I wish to clarify my use of the word *dechurched* for the purposes of this book. I use this term to describe those who have lost a faith that they once valued or have left a body of believers with whom they were once deeply engaged. I limit my exploration further by focusing on those who

1

have felt damaged and alienated amid this process. I cannot judge the authenticity of a person's prior experience with the Christian faith; I can only listen to the pain and disappointment, the questioning and confusion, the anger and even rage that the stories of the dechurched often embody.

Many testimonies of the dechurched are included within the pages of this book. For the sake of confidentiality, I have altered details within these stories and used fictitious names in most circumstances, particularly in those of a sensitive nature. I have occasionally conflated similar accounts in an attempt to protect the privacy of all who have offered me their trust. The histories of this population are difficult to share and to hear. It is a privilege and gift every time I am allowed to enter the pain of the dechurched and participate in its transformation.

At times Jesus concludes his teachings with the admonition, "Listen, then, if you have ears!" (Matthew 11:15). May we take his warning to heart as we seek to enter the world of the dechurched.

PART I

Who Are the Dechurched?

CHAPTER 1

Stories of the Dechurched

Misty grew up in the church. Throughout much of her childhood her uncle sexually molested her. He, too, was a church member. I could hear the cries of a terrified little girl in Misty's voice as she shared her story with me.

Misty confessed, "When I was a child, I was taught at church that God was all-powerful and could do anything for those who truly believed. The pastor reminded us constantly that God answered prayer. He said that God would fulfill the desires of our hearts if we were only faithful. Every Sunday I went to church and asked this all-powerful God to make my uncle stop hurting me."

Misty hesitated. Her facial expression grew distant as she looked back over the years. She finally continued, "Even as I prayed, nothing changed. The abuse never stopped. It finally ended when I left home as a young adult and cut my ties with the entire family."

Then Misty offered a solemn conclusion to her story that I will never forget. She said to me, "I will never again believe in a 'god' who fixes things in our lives here and now. It didn't happen for me, even though I prayed and believed for so long. I had to find a way out of the situation by myself. I had to discover a 'god' within me that was also part of me. That is why I left Christianity and became a Buddhist."

+ + +

I first met Lauri at a discussion group on feminism and Christianity held among Oberlin College students. Each participant had the opportunity to share why she had come. Lauri minced no words when it was her turn to talk. "I am a senior religion major at Oberlin College," she replied, "and I don't have any religion. I decided that it is time to find my faith."

As I got to know Lauri, I learned that her grandfather had been, as she put it, a "hellfire and brimstone" kind of preacher. He was very strict and demanding at home. Among his children, he imparted judgment rather than grace; his presence elicited fear rather than love. Lauri's mother had rejected the faith of her father. As an adult, she vowed that neither she nor any children she might bear would ever set foot in a church. Lauri's father, as well, had his own complaints about Christianity. Both parents had been raised in the church; both left the church wounded.

Lauri's parents consciously raised their daughter in a completely nonreligious environment. At the age of twenty-one, Lauri had never attended a church service in her life. She had been taught since childhood that Christianity was a negative influence to avoid at all costs. In spite of this upbringing, there was a deep spiritual hunger within Lauri's heart. She felt an inner longing to personally address issues that remained profoundly unresolved within her family history. Perhaps it was this same yearning that led Lauri to major in religion at college and attend this interest group on feminism and Christian spirituality.

+ + +

Ruth was the mother of seventeen children. When her spouse died, thirteen children still remained at home. Years later, she added a two-year-old grandson named Steve to her brood. Neither Steve nor his two brothers were able to be cared for by their parents, so each of the three boys was raised by a different relative. Twenty years later, Steve became my husband.

When Steve was in elementary school, he and his Grandma traveled to a little church down the road where they participated in worship services and Sunday school classes. Then, one day, Grandma stopped taking her young grandson to church. He had no idea why they had quit attending. Steve finally asked her what had happened, and she replied, "The church kicked Roger out because of something he did. I just don't think that's how the church should treat people. So we aren't going back there." For several years, they didn't attend church at all.

As Steve entered high school, a new Baptist minister, Pastor Tom, moved to the small rural community in which Ruth and Steve resided. He reached out to the young people in the area as he attempted to establish an ongoing ministry with youth. Through some friends, Steve met Pastor Tom. It wasn't long before Steve was attending every youth event at the church. Grandma Ruth even began coming to church services as well.

Looking back, Steve believes that his experiences as a teenager in the church were critical to his subsequent calling into the ministry. Today, he has served in pastoral ministry for over twenty years.

+ + +

The dechurched are all around us. They are family members; they work in our offices and factories; they live next door or down the street. Their stories are as varied as one can imagine. Some leave the church for years, even decades, and eventually return. Many become openly hostile toward Christianity and cease to care about issues of faith and personal spirituality. Others shove aside painful experiences from their Christian past and embrace radically different belief systems. In church after church, some sit quietly in the sanctuary every sabbath day until one week they disappear.

"What am I doing here? Why do I stay?" is the query that frames a provocative song written by Christian songwriter and vocalist Ken Medema. Nearly every person who commits him- or herself to Christ and the church for the long haul poses these questions along the way. Our answers to them seem muddled and unclear. Times of discouragement and frustration may literally hound us. Many Christians persevere until the day breaks or the clouds pass. Others, however, react differently during such periods of confusion and questioning.

By definition, the dechurched are those who once participated actively in the Christian faith. During the transition from engagement to disengagement, they frequently remain outwardly involved in the events of congregational life while inwardly struggling with fierce questions and pressing issues.

My teenaged daughter, Grace, brought this insight home to me one Sunday at The First Baptist Church of Oberlin as the congregation reflected upon our ministry to the dechurched. "I have lots of friends who are *in church* who do not share the faith of their families," Grace commented. "Some of them say they are atheists. Some of them hate going to church, but their parents make them go. I think we have to remember that there are dechurched people within the church," she concluded.

I was so glad that Grace shared this insight. She did, indeed, know many young people who were expected to participate in congregational life until they were eighteen. At that point, the parents allowed their children to make decisions about faith and church attendance for themselves. We must consider the needs of dechurched teenagers sitting in our church pews Sunday after Sunday. Soon many of them will become adults who leave the church behind.

A youth pastor shares his frustration with me at the number of teens he shepherds through confirmation class who profess no faith whatsoever. "They are so resistant to what they are learning in church," he complains. "It seems at times as if it is the last place they want to be."

I describe the work my husband and I do among dechurched college students to a friend named Judy. Her son John is a reluctant church-going teen. Judy comments, "I'm really glad that you reach out to such young adults, even if your efforts may seem unproductive at times. I hope that when John goes off to college, there will be some place that he can go to work through his issues of faith and doubt. I am not sure that he would be willing to do that, but it would mean a lot to me as a parent to know that there are adults around him who would support him on such a journey."

The dechurched are not found only beyond the confines of our local congregations. No, our churches can also be fertile ground for their presence as well. Whether our congregations consider themselves conservative or liberal, mainline or evangelical, liturgical or spontaneous, charismatic or noncharismatic, dechurched people may be sitting in our pews, struggling with basic issues of faith and its expression.

+ + +

Karen grew up in a suburban church. During her teen years, she began exploring religions outside the Christian faith. A moody, introspective child, Karen secretly struggled with depression and thoughts of suicide. She was afraid to tell anyone about these feelings. Outwardly, she was a high achiever involved in multitudes of extracurricular and church activities. She had lots of friends, but struggled with a deep sense of loneliness. Although Karen had no firsthand exposure to poverty, she possessed an acute concern for the poor and disadvantaged.

People at the church gave money to mission projects and clothing to the needy at Christmas time. The rest of the year, the poor seemed to be far removed from the minds and lives of the materially secure parishioners around Karen. Conversation at the morning coffee hour following Sunday worship revolved around job promotions, vacations, the achievements of everyone's children, and occasionally gossip about someone who wasn't there that day.

Karen was disillusioned as she tried to make sense of the strange juxtaposition of her sensitivities and realities. Her parents were active church members with significant marital problems. Karen longed for them to address the difficulties within their relationship. Yet, to seek counseling was anathema within their social context. Acknowledging personal failure was seen as a sign of weakness, a threat to the sheen of respectability and control that accompanied the middle class lifestyle of Karen's family, church, and community.

Karen hungered for spiritual depth and genuineness. She needed to find a way through her own secret depression. She wanted a religion that would make her feel better, that would help her deal with her personal problems, that would address the real issues of her parents' marriage and the superficiality of her social situation. She believed that faith ought to somehow speak both to the needs of the disadvantaged and the privileges of the advantaged. She didn't want such issues reduced to holiday appeals for donating money to charity. Karen was convinced that any faith worth embracing ought to address each of these pressing concerns in her life.

Karen thus began a search that spanned several years and many faiths. When she left home for college, she visited a church near the campus three times and then stopped attending church altogether. It wasn't long before she quit even thinking about church—or God—and got wrapped up in other pursuits. The process of becoming dechurched, which began for Karen in high school, culminated during her college years as she left both the church and her faith behind.

+ + +

Lonnie spent his high school years struggling with his sexual identity. His family attended a very conservative church where the pastor regularly preached against homosexuality and described all homosexuals as "perverts and distortions of God's truth." A deeply sensitive teen with a keen interest in God, Lonnie felt tortured by his inner secrets. He was convinced that no one around him could be trusted with his struggle, so he faced it alone.

Lonnie sat through church services, week after week, wondering if his life would forever be filled with the utter condemnation of God. He faithfully studied his Sunday school lessons, hoping in his heart that somehow God still loved him. Month by month, year by year, Lonnie went through the motions of his faith, talked the language, attended whatever activities arose, but he kept his inner turmoil to himself.

At eighteen, Lonnie moved away from home. He didn't quite walk away from the church; he just never looked for another church to join. Lonnie was convinced that he wasn't really welcome in the church anyhow. He joined the ranks of the dechurched.

+ + +

Chuck did not grow up in a Christian family. He committed his life to Christ at the age of twelve after a friend at school invited him to church. Chuck quickly became active in the congregation's youth programs. Its youth ministry was expansive and well-developed. Chuck freely shared his musical gifts, read his Bible, and witnessed to his unchurched friends.

Years later as a college student, Chuck shared his story with me: "I loved the church, but there were things that bothered me about it, too. It just seemed so judgmental toward outsiders. I didn't want to become the kind of person that thought I was better than everyone else because I was 'saved' and they weren't." Chuck continued, "The turning point for me came when Brad, one of the kids in the youth group, told the youth pastor that he was gay. Brad was one of the most committed, spiritual kids in the whole bunch. He was always helping others, always praying for people, always studying scripture. Others learned his secret. The church treated him terribly. He was shattered. After that, I just couldn't stay. I couldn't believe that Christians would treat their own this way. I still consider myself a Christian, but the church just isn't for me anymore."

My husband and I invited Chuck to First Baptist Church numerous times during his college years. He never came.

+ + +

Patsy was a preacher's kid. Her dad, Duane, loved a challenge, so he always chose to pastor needy churches in blighted areas. Every church Duane served was a small congregation struggling to make ends meet. Duane's ministry didn't merely engage his own energy; the whole family came as a team to each new setting. They rolled up their sleeves, made the necessary sacrifices, and gave 250 percent of themselves. Patsy's mom, Jane, sang in the choir and organized several of the women's ministries. Patsy's brother, Rod, was gently groomed to follow in his father's pastoral footsteps. Rod was a student leader in the very small but active teen ministry of the church. He engaged a lot of his peers in volunteer efforts that ranged from yard work for senior citizens to food distribution for the hungry.

Patsy, the youngest, was the last to leave the nest. Patsy loved children, so she taught an elementary Sunday school class while she attended high school. She volunteered in the after-school childcare program twice a week. She often ran errands for her parents. Patsy loved being part of a ministry so valuable within the community, yet by the time she reached the age of eighteen, she was tired. Burned out like any retired church member who says, "I've put in my years of being indispensable. It is time for me to rest awhile," Patsy secretly looked forward to leaving home.

When Patsy was eighteen, I met her at a new student orientation event and invited her to our small but vital church. It seemed to bring back childhood memories of attending churches that needed her a little too much. "I don't think I would be interested, but thank you for inviting me," Patsy said. "I just don't want to be indispensable anymore. I just want *to be me*, and I just don't know if I can *be me* in the church."

+ + +

Each of these young people faced a period of becoming dechurched while still actively involved in the life of the church. Each experienced the inevitable shifts and changes that accompany the process of maturing. Their life issues and nagging questions fundamentally impacted their personal beliefs and understandings of the Christian faith and the mission of the church.

Seasoned adults, as well, can continue to serve the church while in the process of becoming dechurched. Shanda's story reflects this reality. She was deeply attached to her church, but struggled with being there at the same time. She enjoyed her work with children, appreciating the openness, tenderness, and exuberance of the preschoolers in her Sunday school class. Their innocent trust in God often renewed Shanda's own faith when it was faltering.

Lately, however, even the children could not reach this faithful church worker. Shanda often found herself becoming angry during worship services for no apparent reason. Her tolerance for the little glitches and wrinkles of ordinary life was waning. Her patience was wearing thin, even with the children's ministry that she so deeply loved.

Eventually, Shanda began to realize that her problems weren't really about church at all; instead, they were issues surfacing within herself. When Shanda's mother died unexpectedly, she was thrown into a tailspin of grief, despondency, and weekly nightmares. Issues from childhood that she had neatly tucked into a box, far removed from her conscious mind, came flooding back into her consciousness. She hardly knew how to deal with all that was happening inside. Who could she talk to?

Everyone at church seemed busy just "praising the Lord." Their testimonies were always so neat and tidy. Yes, they had come through hard times; they had fought the good fight and won. They had subdued Satan, the roaring lion that sought to devour them. But now it was Shanda's turn to feel devoured. She quietly wondered, "Who do these people talk to when they are *in the middle of the crisis*, not testifying about getting to the other side?" Shanda had no idea.

Shanda remained in the church, continuing her children's ministry. Meanwhile, she distanced herself from other activities. She knew the language of the church. She could shout her praises, sing her choruses, wave her arms, and utter her amen's. She could prepare her Sunday school lessons and offer all the appropriate answers to her young students' questions. Inside, however, Shanda was struggling, wrestling, hurting, and crying. The answers she parroted back to others felt hollow, and relevant to everyone but herself. Shanda felt a million miles removed from both the church and the faith in which she had invested her whole life. This faithful Christian and children's worker was one step away from becoming dechurched.

+ + +

Those of us within the church must not neglect to notice the dechurched among us. These fellow sojourners are not always outside our doors. Sometimes they are only a few feet away in the same pew. They may stay and suffer silently, remaining in the church for a host of reasons. Some may still feel connected to their faith in the midst of difficult seasons of doubt and disbelief, tragedy and despair. Others may stay for reasons of belonging, for the power or security their church roles give them, or even out of timidity about acting on their true feelings and actually leaving. Some may be caught up in people-pleasing to such an extent that they care more about their image at church than the reality in their own souls. Many who stay withdraw emotionally in profound yet often unspoken ways.

Others quietly leave. They take off without offering any external indication of their problems or struggles. Those of us who remain in the church must be like the shepherd pursuing that one sheep who wanders away from the ninety-nine. Someone must reach out to people like Karen, Lonnie, Chuck, and Shanda. A friend or pastor must ask, "What are you feeling? What do you need to talk about? What has been happening in your life? What are the struggles of your faith?" Too often an absence or withdrawal is never addressed. Too easily, such people silently slip off the church rolls after a season as "inactive members."

The dechurched in our pews someday become the dechurched in our neighborhoods, workplaces, and families. One way we can stem the exodus is to create safe spaces within the church for those who face crises of faith and periods of disbelief. Perhaps the church can then be a sanctuary for the wounded and a road station for the lost among its own.

CHAPTER 2

Jesus and the Dechurched

I have read many books on evangelism in my life and tried many methods of local church outreach. Very few, in fact, have been helpful to the ministry God has given me among the dechurched. There is a simple reason for this. Strategies for contemporary evangelism draw clear demarcations between "the saved" and "the unsaved," the Christian and the non-Christian. An unspoken yet primary assumption undergirds outreach among "the unsaved": *Such people have never really heard or embraced the gospel of Jesus Christ.* According to this model, the evangelist offers "the unsaved" their first genuine introduction to Christianity. The potential convert has the opportunity to accept or reject the message delivered. It is thus assumed that "the unsaved" person in question explores Christianity with a clean slate and no prior Christian experience.

However, this premise can only be true among those frequently described in church growth literature as "the unchurched." According to such writings, the unchurched are defined as those who have never heard or received the good news of Jesus Christ. Their only exposure to Christianity on a personal level may be what they have absorbed through popular culture or other secondary sources. The unchurched may chafe against commitment to Christ and prefer retaining control over their own lives for a host of reasons. They may experience prejudices and biases about Christianity. They may be indifferent or hostile to the Christian message, but they do not bring a negative experience of Christianity to the exploration of faith.

The dechurched, on the other hand, bring a very full slate to their lack of engagement with Christianity or the church. They may have been raised in an intense Christian environment against which they rebelled and which they later rejected. They may have attended church three or four times a week as children and memorized lots of Bible verses. Many have served the church faithfully for years of their adult lives. Some experienced life-changing conversions at points of genuine crisis. The stories of the dechurched are different than those of the unchurched, as are their needs for ministry and pastoral care.

Rarely is any distinction made in contemporary models of outreach between the unchurched and the dechurched, yet profound differences between these groups exist and must be recognized. Many of the dechurched have legitimate reasons for rejecting what they once understood Christianity to be. Many have been wounded "in the name of God."

The dechurched represent a potent challenge to the church. They are among the church's strongest critics because they are outsiders who were once insiders. Their criticism is often strident, rooted in honest pain about the nature and witness of the contemporary church. At times their passionate vision of what Christianity *ought to be* drives them away from the faith that they see practiced. Even though they rarely know it and would scarcely believe it, the dechurched hold a key to a renewed vision of the church. Tragically, the church hardly notices.

Jesus teaches us what a ministry among the dechurched can be. His three years of public ministry revolved in large part around an outreach to the de-synagogued. A sharp distinction existed between those who meticulously followed the details of the Jewish law and those who did not. Numerous Israelites fell short of such obedience. Some were morally suspect. Others were rendered unclean by disease, thus preventing their full participation in religious life and ritual. Still others had wandered far from their spiritual heritage. Yet Jesus had a special love for those who found themselves on the fringes of institutional religious practice.

In spite of a few notable exceptions when Jesus ministered among the Gentile and Samaritan populations, his primary calling was to Israel and his own people, the Jews. The religious leaders did not appreciate the company that Jesus kept. They constantly criticized him for his choice of friends. "This man welcomes sinners and eats with them," the Pharisees and teachers of the law complained (Luke 15:2, NRSV).

Numerous gospel stories illustrate the love of Jesus for the de-synagogued. Jesus allowed a sinful woman to anoint him at a public gathering in the home of a Pharisee. Another Pharisee silently grumbled, "If this man really were a prophet, he would know who this woman is who is touching him; he would know what kind of sinful life she lives!" (Luke 7:39). In contrast to the Pharisee's unspoken judgment, Jesus graciously accepted the woman's gift.

On another occasion, Jesus felt the tentative touch of a bleeding woman, infirm for many years. The gospel of Luke identified her condition as an "issue of blood," or constant menstrual flow. According to Jewish teaching, such a condition rendered the woman perpetually unclean and unable to share in the fullness of religious life within her community. The Levitical law stated:

> If a woman has a flow of blood for several days outside her monthly period or if her flow continues beyond her regular period, she remains unclean as long as the flow continues, just as she is during her monthly period. Any bed on which she lies and anything on which she sits during this time is unclean. Anyone who touches them is unclean and must wash his clothes and take a bath; he remains unclean until evening. After her flow stops, she must wait seven days, and then she will be ritually clean. On the eighth day she shall take two doves or two pigeons to the priest at the entrance of the Tent of the Lord's presence. The priest shall offer one of them as a sin offering and the other as a burnt offering, and in this way he will perform the ritual of purification for her. The Lord told Moses to warn the people of Israel about their uncleanness, so that they would not defile the Tent of

his presence, which was in the middle of the camp. If they
did, they would be killed. (Leviticus 15:25–31)

It was an enormous risk for such a woman to touch even the
hem of Jesus' garment. As she did so, power went out from Jesus,
and the woman's bleeding ceased. "Who touched me?" Jesus asked.
Everyone in the crowd initially denied the act. Peter, the disciple of
Jesus, explained, "Master, the people are all around you and crowding
in on you" (Luke 8:45). Yet Jesus was convinced that someone had
reached out for him. Soon after this, the woman hesitantly came
forward and confessed her deed. She threw herself at Jesus' feet,
begging for mercy. He blessed her, saying, "My daughter, your faith
has made you well. Go in peace" (Luke 8:48).

In another story, Jesus invited himself to the house of Zacchaeus,
a tax collector (Luke 19:1–10). Tax collectors were considered
notoriously dishonest. They were seen as traitors who had
compromised their own people in order to profit from the Roman
occupation of Israel. Zacchaeus was no exception to this stereotype.
By the time Jesus left his home, Zacchaeus had agreed to give to
the poor much of what he had gained fraudulently and to pay back
fourfold those whom he had cheated.

Many other stories of Jesus and the de-synagogued fill the gospels.
Jesus refused to condemn a woman caught in the act of adultery,
even as her male captors yearned to stone her to death (John 8:1–
11). Instead, he sent her away with words of encouragement, "Go,
but do not sin again" (John 8:11b). Jesus healed the demoniac from
Gerasa, a man so insane and violent that the villagers kept him in
chains outside the town (Luke 8:26–39). When the man begged to
travel with Jesus and his disciples, Jesus sent him back to testify
among the very neighbors who had shunned him (Luke 8:39). The
mentally ill, the physically infirm, the morally suspect, the ritually
unclean, the exploitive and the exploited—all of these were among
the friends and followers of Jesus.

The uncleanliness and sinfulness of Jesus' friends was a barrier
to their participation in first-century Jewish life. The strictest
followers of the law did not believe that these people were "worthy"
to receive God's unqualified favor and abundant blessing. The de-
synagogued were not welcomed into the community of faith by

those generally recognized as the most faithful. Was part of the brokenness that Jesus healed perhaps the alienation that these outsiders experienced from the faith of their ancestors?

Jesus' ministry to this population represented an enormous challenge to the religious leaders of his day. There was resistance to Jesus' choice of relationships. There was resistance to the inclusion of such individuals in God's realm. There was resistance to Jesus himself.

The same challenges that Jesus faced confront the contemporary church. Indeed, the church represents Christ as his body on earth. It is incumbent upon us, therefore, to minister after the example of our Lord and Savior. This inevitably leads us to experience God's pain and pathos for the dechurched of our own time.

CHAPTER 3

The Parables of the Lost

One day, Jesus invited a man named Simon to go fishing (Luke 5:1–11). The previous night of work had been a wasted effort, producing next to nothing for the fisherman. Yet Jesus urged Simon to go out again and see what happened, this time accompanied by Jesus. Simon complied, and it wasn't long before the boat nearly sank under the weight of a remarkable catch (Luke 5:5–7).

This was a fishing expedition not to be forgotten. Simon was stricken with more than amazement at his success. He cried out to Jesus, "Go away from me, Lord. I am a sinful man!" (Luke 5:8b). Jesus did not leave. He stayed with Simon and urged him to finish his job, row the boat to shore, then come and follow him. Jesus offered Simon one cryptic comment, which the fisherman probably did not understand at the time. He told Simon, "Do not be afraid; from now on you will be catching people" (Luke 5:10b, NRSV).

Jesus enlisted Simon and the other disciples he had gathered unto himself in the lost and found business. They were not to look for fish, fame, or fortune. The followers of Jesus were sent out to search for *people,* human beings who had become lost and needed the compassionate touch of others if they were to be found.

In the gospel of Luke, Jesus tells three parables, or stories, about his search for the lost. The imagery itself is explosive. Jesus compares God's searching heart to the efforts of a faithful shepherd doggedly pursuing one wandering sheep, a pushy housekeeper turning her home upside down to recover a precious lost coin, and a wounded father anxiously waiting for his lost son to return home.

The three portraits painted in these parables embody the tensions each of us face in our relationships with the lost today. We struggle with the contradiction between doing everything in our power to find the lost, as the shepherd and the housekeeper do, or simply waiting for the lost to find themselves, even as the patient father must. We are forced to live amid the paradox of these two realities. The lost must be sought; someone must call them by name and speak to them words of love and welcome. Yet the lost must also be relinquished into the hands of God. At times they must be left alone to exhaust their human resources and face their own lostness.

The immediate context for Jesus' parables about the lost is critical to the understanding of the text. These three stories were told in direct response to the criticism that Jesus received from the Pharisees and the teachers of the law regarding the company he kept. The guardians of institutional religion bitterly complained, "This man welcomes sinners and eats with them!" (Luke 15:2). The outcasts of whom these religious leaders spoke were not Gentiles. Rather, they were Jews whose birthrights offered them a place of welcome within Jewish life, yet whose infirmities, lifestyles, disabilities, or rebelliousness did not.

Amid the brokenness and pain of these lost ones, Jesus envisioned healing and renewal, even transformation. He called out their potential and promise and gave them an opportunity to make dynamic commitments to the reign of God that he proclaimed.

The Parable of the Lost Sheep

The parables of the lost begin with the story of the determined shepherd who pursues his one lost sheep while trusting that the ninety-nine others will remain safe during his search. This image is both earthy and winsome. It is one of a conscientious laborer expending the extra effort required by the demands of his job. It is also one of a lover doing the heart-work that his vocation demands.

"Suppose one of you has a hundred sheep and loses one of them—what does he do? He leaves the other ninety-nine sheep in the pasture and goes looking for the one that got lost until he finds it. When he finds it, he is so happy that he puts it on his shoulders and carries it back home. Then he calls his friends and neighbors together and says to them, 'I am so happy I found my lost sheep. Let us celebrate!' In the same way, I tell you, there will be more joy in heaven over one sinner who repents than over ninety-nine respectable people who do not need to repent." (Luke 15:4–7)

+ + +

My husband and I have served The First Baptist Church of Oberlin for many years. Steve was called to the church as its pastor when he graduated from seminary in 1979. I served alongside him first as pastor's wife, then beginning in 1983 as pastoral associate, and finally as copastor since 1985.

When we first came to the church, the congregation had twelve active members, ten of whom were retired. They had considered closing their doors and returning ownership of the building to the Ohio Baptist Convention. Yet one church member, Bob Thomas, outlined another alternative that eventually gained the attention of all twelve. Bob suggested that the church ask the state leaders for help in hiring a young, full-time pastor for a two-year assignment. If the church was not completely self-supporting within two years, it would then close its doors. If the two years of renewed effort produced significant growth, then the church would continue to remain a viable presence in the Oberlin community.

The deal was accepted by both the congregation and the staff of the Ohio Baptist Convention. With this two-year agreement in place, Steve became the church's pastor. Together with our two small children, we came to Oberlin as hands-on partners in this ministry of rebuilding the congregation. The first two years were exhilarating and exhausting as attendance climbed from twelve toward seventy.

The numbers of active parishioners eventually began to settle around fifty, sometimes forty during lean years. The church continued its significant ministry to Oberlin College students that it had carried on for decades. This work on campus involved the constant welcome of new students as well as the endless departure of graduates. The congregation also found itself reaching out to newcomers in the community and people in crisis. At times, the nonstudent population was as transient, or more so, than the students who stayed for four or five years!

Steve and I prayed constantly for church growth. In our hearts, we envisioned a full sanctuary, a packed schedule of activities, and a high level of energy. We prayed for the countless people we believed would benefit from participating in the life of the church. Many of them never walked through the doors. We offered sustained seasons of prayer for particular visitors so that they might become more deeply engaged in the life and ministry of the church. Sometimes they did and sometimes they didn't.

After seventeen years of such praying, I stepped back and questioned my vision of church growth. I began praying instead for wisdom about my prayers for church growth. I knew that First Baptist was a "sending" church, mentoring young people who would provide leadership in other congregations after they graduated. I also realized that the church reached out to many beyond its doors who might never step into any church, particularly a Baptist church. There was still much that eluded me about this pesky prayer and my unending yearning for more sheep to join the flock. For two years, I sought the wisdom to understand why this prayer continued to seem unanswered.

As I took my morning walk one day, I began praying once again for wisdom regarding the growth of the church. At first it seemed like just another one of the numerous times I had uttered the same prayer, but this day was different. The voice of the Holy One pierced my heart with these unforgettable words: "I have sent you to the one and not the ninety-nine. But, oh, how the angels in heaven rejoice when that one who was lost is found!"

That was it. That was the whole thing. That was the vision I had sought for nineteen years while I patiently ministered in Oberlin. As I marveled at these words and began meditating on them, I turned to this parable of the determined shepherd who sought his one lost sheep, leaving the ninety-nine behind, trusting that the others would all be safe without him.

Faces of real people flooded my thoughts. Louie, who had spent most of his adult life in prison and is now an active, participating, ministering part of the congregation. Cassie, who lives in a nursing home eleven miles away and rarely gets out if folks at church don't pick her up for activities and events. Jan, Sarah, Lynn, Carl, and so many others who were dechurched for some time before discovering First Baptist Church. Still more names came to mind—young adults who asked too many questions in Sunday school when they were growing up; college students on the brink of spiritual awakenings; gentle, tortured souls struggling with mental illness; outcasts from other churches; ones who had been divorced; others whose children had gone astray; still others who had lost a spouse to lingering illness; some who wondered if they could ever believe again. On and on the images flashed through my mind. I was overcome with the directness of God's message: "I have sent you to the one and not the ninety-nine."

I realized that the vast majority of ministry that Steve and I do revolves around "the one" rather than the ninety-nine. We never quite follow the beaten path of institutional religion or denominational practice. We search out the voices that are rarely heard. We struggle with issues that few people are eager to discuss. We make friends with those living on the margins. We often find ourselves more at home on the periphery of the church than with those solidly rooted in mainstream church life. Even after nearly two decades of ministry together, our passion to reach outsiders has not abated.

To be truthful, I often look at the churches that minister to the ninety-nine with a touch of envy. I hate those clergy meetings where the first question another pastor always asks is, "How many new members have you taken in this year?" or "How big is your congregation?" One of my secret longings is to have a church facility that houses at least two toilet stalls per sex and one drinking fountain. When I visit other churches, I continually marvel at the existence of church drinking fountains.

I read the church newsletters of congregations that raise a quarter of a million dollars for their capital campaigns in a few months' time. Then I look at what a difference $2,000 can make to the budget of First Baptist Church in an entire year. I note the long lists of new members that are regularly added to the flock elsewhere. I look around at the fifty faces I see each Sunday and ruefully note my rusty prayers.

Yet in an instant, my perspective was radically altered. The ninety-nine seemed like the solid church folk who knew what they believed and would continue their lives of faith with minimal direction. The one lost sheep, however, needed the special attention of the shepherd. Without the shepherd's committed efforts, this one would remain hopelessly lost and never find the way home.

Ministry to "the one" is time intensive, profound, and filled with contradictions. "The one" often has more questions and doubts than the ninety-nine combined. "The one" has buried sorrows that require patience and gentleness to unearth and heal. "The one" may be bent on going his or her own direction, even if it means wandering far from the flock for an indefinite period of time.

For Jesus, "the one" surely included the de-synagogued. For me, "the one" includes the dechurched, that person who once believed that the church and the life of faith were important, but no longer does. "The one" is somehow off the beaten trail, perhaps too unorthodox for the ninety-nine, too needy, too confused, or even too cynical. Jesus is clear. "The one" will not be found without the dogged pursuit of the determined shepherd, the faithful pastor, the helpful neighbor, the loving friend, or the persevering spouse.

"But, oh, how the angels rejoice when that one who was lost is found!" God reminded me that day on my morning walk. The shepherd in the parable placed the lost sheep on his back when it was recovered and took it home to the village for a celebration. In small towns of ancient times, a shepherd often tended the flock of the entire village. The joy of finding the one lost sheep belonged to the gathered community, not just the single shepherd. When the lost was found, the whole people of God appropriately threw a party.

Unfortunately, the Pharisees and teachers of the law weren't terribly interested in joining Jesus in this celebration of inclusion and welcome. Neither are many in the church today. The drama continues.

The Parable of the Lost Coin

The second parable Jesus recounts in this series of stories about seeking the lost of Israel is found nowhere else but in the gospel of Luke. It is the shortest of the three illustrations as well as the most compact in detail. The image of God that Jesus employs is nothing less than stunning; it is that of a diligent female housekeeper looking persistently for her precious lost coin.

> "Or suppose a woman who has ten silver coins loses one of them—what does she do? She lights a lamp, sweeps her house, and looks carefully everywhere until she finds it. When she finds it, she calls her friends and neighbors together, and says to them, 'I am so happy I found the coin I lost. Let us celebrate!' In the same way, I tell you, the angels of God rejoice over one sinner who repents." (Luke 15:8–10)

Our family lived for seven years in a house right across the street from the church. A widow lived next door, and her grandson Jake often came to visit. He was close in age to our oldest daughter, and he always looked forward to spending plenty of time at our house playing with our three girls when he visited his grandmother.

One day, Jake came over while my husband was vacuuming. He looked at Steve in utter astonishment and said, "You vacuum?" Steve looked up from his work and replied in a matter-of-fact way, "Yes, I vacuum." To Steve, this was nothing particularly unusual.

Jake continued in disbelief. "You vacuum, you cook, you do dishes. What else do you do?"

It finally occurred to Steve that Jake was shocked to see a man doing what he had been raised to consider as solely "women's work." Jake simply could not wrap his mind around the concept of a man vacuuming the house. So it is with many of us as we explore this second parable about the lost. How many church folk resist imagining God as a plucky female housekeeper, sweeping carefully until she finds her special lost coin? Such a rendering of God is considered as inappropriate as a man vacuuming seemed to Jake.

Our rigid gender roles can easily constrict our ability to see or imagine anything beyond the constructs that we have previously been taught. Both this parable and the illustration about Jake demonstrate important points about God. Many of us have fixed images of the Divine that are predominantly or even exclusively male. Yet Jesus uses three images in the parables of Luke 15: the gentle, determined shepherd; the energetic, persistent housekeeper; and the wounded, patient father. In each of these stories, Jesus forcefully responds to the criticism of the Pharisees and the teachers of the law regarding the company he keeps, particularly his friendships among those Jews on the fringes of institutional religion.

Each of the images for God in these parables is earthy and commonplace in some respects. Yet there is nothing commonplace about these images when they are used as a reference to the love of God for the lost. To see God's love for the de-synagogued or the dechurched described as that of a shepherd, housekeeper, or father is indeed profound.

Predictably, the second parable of this group is the most neglected of the three. The parable of the lost sheep is also recounted in Matthew's gospel (Matthew 18:12–14). The imagery of Jesus as the Good Shepherd is alluded to again in the gospel of John (John 10:1–18). The third parable, the story of the prodigal son, has captured the imaginations of storytellers worldwide. Its text has spawned numerous Christian musicals, dramas, poems, and narratives. The imagery for the Holy One in the first and last parables is male. Here, in this second parable, it is female. Further, there are no references in the parable of the lost coin to any males at all, whether husband, son, or other relative.

Commentators for centuries have explained this housekeeper reference to God by looking back at the Christian church's formulation of the Trinity as Father, Son, and Holy Spirit. They have often linked each story to a particular aspect of the Trinity. The parable of the lost sheep referred to Jesus, the Good Shepherd. The parable of the lost son referred to God the Father. By elimination, the parable of the lost coin must have referred to the Holy Spirit.

The use of feminine imagery for the Holy Spirit is considered more palatable than imagining God in female terms, or so this line of thinking proceeds. In defense of such an interpretation, there are valid reasons to relate this second parable to the work of the Holy Spirit. The Hebrew word *ruach,* which is the term used for the Holy Spirit, is feminine. The word for Holy Spirit is neutered in the Greek (*pneuma*) and made masculine in Latin biblical translations.

Indeed, the Holy Spirit functions as the birthing agent of the Godhead. The Spirit hovers over the waters to form order from chaos in Genesis 1. The Spirit inspires prophets to speak God's word throughout the texts of Isaiah, Jeremiah, Micah, and many others.

The Spirit comes upon Mary the mother of Jesus, causing her to conceive without "knowing" a man (Luke 1:26–37). The Spirit descends on Jews and Gentiles alike, birthing the church in the book of Acts (Acts 2:1–13; 10). The Spirit searches our hearts as well as the deep things of God (1 Corinthians 2:10). The Spirit convicts, comforts, and bears witness to the truth (John 14:16–17, 26; 15:26; 16:7–15). The Holy Spirit, in fact, sweeps through us and exposes that which we otherwise might not see within ourselves, even insights as small as a lost coin buried in the corner of a house.

In spite of all this parallelism, however, there are equally valid reasons to reject this method of interpreting these three parables of the lost. To limit our understanding of this second parable to a metaphor for the work of the Holy Spirit in the life of a believer is to neglect both the context for this story and the likely intent of Jesus as he offers three different illustrations to make one critical point. If we neatly separate these stories, using a Trinitarian formula that developed as Christian theology emerged, we read back into the text many concepts that arose later within church history.

What was it that Jesus sought to communicate to the Pharisees and teachers of the law as he spoke? Surely he was not offering a sophisticated monologue on the nature and mission of the Trinity. To limit our understanding of this parable to imagery of the Holy Spirit is to reinforce our tendency to see God one-dimensionally when the Bible offers us numerous names and images for the Holy One. We quickly wind up in the same league with Jake, who cannot move out of his rigid understandings of what men can and cannot do.

As we explore the parable of the lost coin more deeply, we notice that the housekeeper is persistent and aggressive in the search for her precious coin. She does not give up, even when the search seems to be fruitless. Her tenacity, ultimately, is the key to her victory. Her commitment to success is so stubborn it seems almost irritating.

The first two parables embody God's love for the lost as well as the necessity of seeking them out, but this is not the whole story. When all is said and done, the lost must also come to their senses and find themselves. It is this reality that permeates the last parable Jesus tells his skeptical audience.

The Parable of the Lost Sons

"There was once a man who had two sons. The younger one said to him, 'Father, give me my share of the property now.' So the man divided his property between his two sons. After a few days the younger son sold his part of the property and left home with the money. He went to a country far away, where he wasted his money in reckless living. He spent everything he had. Then a severe famine spread over that country, and he was left without a thing. So he went to work for one of the citizens of that country, who sent him out to his farm to take care of the pigs. He wished he could fill himself with the bean pods the pigs ate, but no one gave him anything to eat. At last he came to his senses and said, 'All my father's hired workers have more than they can eat, and here I am about to starve! I will get up and go to my father and say, "Father, I have sinned against God and against you. I am no longer fit to be called your son; treat me as one of your hired workers."' So he got up and started back to his father. He was still a long way from home when his father saw him; his heart was filled with pity, and he ran, threw his arms around his son, and kissed him. 'Father,' the son said, 'I have sinned against God and against you. I am no longer fit to be called your son.' But the father called to his servants. 'Hurry!' he said. 'Bring the best robe and put it on him. Put a ring on his finger and shoes on his feet. Then go and get the prize calf and kill it, and let us celebrate with a feast! For this son of mine was dead, but now he is alive; he was lost, but now he has been found.' And so the feasting began." (Luke 15:11–24)

For years, I struggled to find myself within the parable of the prodigal son. Whenever I heard an exposition of the text, the story was triumphantly related to the most rebellious, foolish sinner around with the juiciest testimony of faith. Here was a son who had the pluck to ask his father for his inheritance in advance, then had the nerve to go out and waste the whole sum on riotous living.

I just couldn't relate to the son's choices at all. If anything, I had been the model child growing up. My friends in college teased me when they learned that I had only seen two R-rated movies (both very poignant movies with profound themes) after eighteen years of life. I had never used foul language, experimented with alcohol or other drugs, cheated on tests, or done much of anything particularly worthy of gossip or innuendo. Some college friends were eager to pollute my stellar record. Others were basically dumbfounded that I had navigated the turbulent decade of the 1960s in such a fashion.

So, the story of the prodigal son simply did not speak to me. Of course, I could relate to this young man's inability to measure up to his father's expectations. I identified with the temptations of making foolish decisions or avoiding serious commitments. But the real energy of the parable, it always seemed, was found in the despicable acts of the son, his powerful moment of repentance, and the father's weary yet ultimately triumphant love.

It wasn't until I reached my thirties that I realized there were *two* lost sons in this parable, not one. I was more like the second than the first. The main character of the story, it always seemed, was the prodigal son, the one with the unsavory story of sin and the glorious story of redemption. The shadowy figure of the elder son, however, remained unnoticed and unnamed. Yet it was he who eventually became my source of identification with this parable.

> "In the meantime the older son was out in the field. On his way back, when he came close to the house, he heard the music and dancing. So he called one of the servants and asked him, 'What's going on?' 'Your brother has come back home,' the servant answered, 'and your father has killed the prize calf, because he got him back safe and sound.' The older brother was so angry that he would not go into the house; so his father came out and begged him to come in. But he spoke back to his father, 'Look, all these years I have worked for you like a slave, and I have never disobeyed your orders. What have you given me? Not even a goat for me to have a feast with my friends! But this son of yours wasted all your property on prostitutes, and when he comes back home,

you kill the prize calf for him!'"My son,' the father answered, 'you are always here with me, and everything I have is yours. But we have to celebrate and be happy, because your brother was dead, but now he is alive; he was lost, but now he has been found.'" (Luke 15:25–32)

The prodigal son took the path of most resistance as he moved from childhood to adulthood. He was pushy, self-absorbed, and rebellious to the point of utter ruin. The elder son took the path of least resistance as he moved from childhood to adulthood. He was complacent, pleasing, and self-sacrificing to the point of utter ruin. His own demise was not as apparent or showy as that of his brother. Yet even as he worked faithfully for his father, his service was characterized by resentment and anger rather than contentment and generosity. His life was motivated by duty rather than love. He was every bit as lost as his brother, yet nobody really noticed. So it is among the lost, even today.

The patient father is a major player in this taut drama. He complies with his younger son's request for an advance of his inheritance. The father waits out the period when his foolish son wanders off with all his father's hard-earned cash, squandering it endlessly on the very pleasures of which his father disapproved. We can almost feel the wounded heart of the patient father as he wonders and waits. The question must surely have haunted his days, What has become of my son?

The boy continues his wayward path until the day he hits rock bottom. He is sitting among the pigs whose pens he has been hired to clean. According to Jewish law, pigs are unclean animals (Leviticus 11:7–8). The son comes to his senses and says to himself, "All my father's hired workers have more than they can eat, and here I am about to starve! I will get up and go to my father and say, 'Father, I have sinned against God and against you. I am no longer fit to be called your son; treat me as one of your hired workers.'" (Luke 15:17–19). So, at long last, the son sets out for the journey home. He takes along a healthy dose of contrition, hoping that he can at least be received as a servant if not as a son.

When the young man nears his father's house, the father recognizes him from a distance. Could this be the boy whose fate had filled the father's thoughts and imagination for days, months, and maybe even years? The father is so joyful to have his son home again, he puts aside all memory of the boy's long absence and foolish behavior. The father calls his servants and orders them to prepare a huge feast and celebration.

The elder brother, however, is furious. Perhaps for the first time in his life, he tells his father what he truly thinks. The father remains undeterred from his plan, and he once again invites his elder son to fully participate in his joy. "'My son,' the father answered, 'you are always here with me, and everything I have is yours. But we had to celebrate and be happy, because your brother was dead, but now he is alive; he was lost, but now he has been found.'" (Luke 15:31–32).

The story ends.

This final parable of Jesus provides the ultimate punch line among his three stories about the lost. The elder son is reminiscent of the Pharisees and teachers of the law. They refuse to celebrate with Jesus over the de-synagogued whom he welcomes. They won't rejoice over the sinners and tax collectors Jesus befriends. They simply reject the party God is planning.

The adulterous woman, the demon-possessed, the rogue tax collector, the plotting Zealot—each of these whom Jesus loves has a story worthy of the headlines. They are all prodigals winding their ways home. The elder son, on the other hand, remains in the shadows, unwilling to participate in the startling work of God.

This last parable underscores the crucial point that the lost, ultimately, have to come to their own senses and find themselves. The father in this story does not dash out in pursuit of his son as the boy squanders his whole inheritance. Instead, the wounded father patiently waits, stoking the fires of his deep love for his offspring while relinquishing his control over that same child's behavior. It is a poignant image that relates to the journey that each one of us travels.

The father invites his resentful elder son to the party but does not force him to come. It is in the hands of this lost son, as well, to discover that his service is dutiful but nonetheless impure, his heart is given to service but not to compassion, and his life is not where it needs to be.

"Come, celebrate with me!" Jesus cries out in each of these three parables about the lost. If the Holy One gently tends to the birds of the air and the lilies of the field (Matthew 6:26–30), it is a virtual certainty that the life of each lost one is of inestimable worth to God. Once again, the refrain rings in my ears, "I have sent you to the one and not the ninety-nine. But, oh, how the angels in heaven rejoice when that one who was lost is finally found!"

PART II

Why Are People Dechurched?

CHAPTER 4

Abused in God's Name

The situations that lead people to experience the state of lostness that Jesus describes in the parables of Luke 15 are often complicated. I cannot begin to address every possible circumstance, but certain themes have emerged repeatedly in my twenty years of working among the dechurched. A pastor recently asked me, "How do you deal with the person who left the church because another parishioner never returned their favorite pan after a potluck?" I really don't confront injuries of such a trivial nature in this book. Conversely, small issues sometimes trigger or mask much larger issues that are harder to name and address. It is easier to leave the church over a missing dish than over something substantial, profound, and persistently troubling.

Years ago, I was asked to lead an AIDS support group. Nearly everyone who came identified himself or herself as a Christian. While the main thrust of the effort was to reach Oberlin families affected by a diagnosis of AIDS among themselves or their loved ones, very few local citizens participated. Others came from miles away to attend this group in order to share their struggles while maintaining their anonymity.

Carol's husband died from complications of AIDS. The family kept the nature of his disease secret from next-door neighbors and relatives to the end. Two gay sons of Jim and Jane died of AIDS a few years apart. Wanda faced fresh grief over the recent death of her twenty-seven-year-old son. Tammy took her drug-addicted nephew into her home for his final months rather than allow him to die on the city streets.

One day, I asked the Christian members of this group how their churches had supported them through the slow and agonizing deaths of their loved ones. They looked startled as if they found my question odd. Jim and Jane replied, "We could never talk to our pastor about this. He preaches against homosexuals all the time!" Wanda quietly confessed, "The church would never have accepted my son in his final months. It was better to face this alone."

Around the room, I heard the same story again and again. My heart grieved to realize that the church, which was important to nearly every person there, did not provide a safe haven for these caregivers and survivors. It was not a refuge where these weary, heartbroken individuals could speak the truth of their lives and discover unconditional love. Instead, the church was a place to don guarded masks and wear them constantly.

In spite of an inability to be honest in the church, these caregivers still found comfort in their faith. They were able to separate the judgment of Christians from the strength that God provided to help them get through their experiences. Not all individuals are this capable of overlooking the church's failure to offer compassion. Others in similar situations have turned away from Christianity after being rejected by Christians during times when they most needed their support. This continues to happen to many families and individuals facing the diagnosis of AIDS. Institutionalized attitudes of condemnation prevent many from encountering Christ's love through his followers.

+ + +

Not only do dechurched people experience institutional rejection or abuse, but some face personal abuse at the hands of professing Christians who live exemplary public lives while maintaining abusive private lives. All abuse—whether sexual, physical, emotional, or intellectual (such as mind control)—has consequences of a profoundly spiritual nature. Abuse can be structural, buttressing social patterns or prejudices. It can also be personal and individualized. When an abuser claims to follow Christ, the abused receives destructive messages about God, the church, and the life of faith itself.

Aileen faced this contradiction between public piety and private abuse in her own family life. She was raised among several siblings. Her parents frequently relocated because her father was an itinerant evangelist and pastoral counselor. He set up his ministry in one location for a while and then moved again. Wherever he traveled, he seemed to be well respected and well received. Aileen's mother was a good-hearted, self-sacrificing woman with a tremendous admiration and respect for her preacher-husband. She felt that no sacrifice was too great as long as she was supporting her husband's calling as a man of God.

Young Aileen loved her family deeply. Her parents were strict, yet this did not seem excessively burdensome to either Aileen or her siblings. As the years passed, however, this strictness escalated into harsh punishments characterized by physical violence and verbal humiliation. When Aileen and her siblings reached their teen years, her father brutally paddled the children bare-bottomed at any seeming infraction of his rules. Aileen's self-consciousness increased with the onset of adolescence. She suspected that sexual innuendos laced these punishments.

It wasn't long before Aileen's father began making inappropriate comments to her about her changing body. She ignored them at first, but he became more persistent. One day her father suggested that he could offer her the sexual experience she would need to prepare her for marriage someday. She was terrified. From that point on, she began searching for ways to avoid being at home alone with her father. She couldn't imagine telling her mother what had happened; her mother would never believe her. Aileen was sure the problem must be something that she herself had done. What could it be?

Not only did Aileen's fear of her father increase with each sexual comment and disciplinary incident, but Aileen also became angry with God. How could her father preach about the love of God in front of a congregation on Sunday and act the way he did on Tuesday and Wednesday? Aileen struggled intensely with her family secrets. On the one hand, church was a refuge for her, a place where she could fold into the crowds of people and avoid the close interpersonal contact with her father that she faced everyday at home. On the other hand, the happy preacher's family displayed on Sunday mornings seemed like a farce to her. Church folk often commented on what "good kids" Aileen and her siblings were and how obedient they were to their parents. If they only knew.

The image of Christ in abusers such as Aileen's father is not merely distorted by human imperfections. The Christ-image is disfigured by the severe unresolved problems of abusive adults. Sometimes inappropriate behavior reflects the abuser's own childhood trauma that was never adequately addressed. Other times it may be tied to symptoms of untreated mental illness in a family member. Sometimes it is neither. Regardless, the growing child faces great obstacles to discerning the beauty and freedom of the gospel within a home where Christian faith is supposedly practiced yet abuse remains closeted and denied.

+ + +

Cult-like religious organizations harbor manipulative and abusive patterns of relationship. Individuals often experience threats of ostracism and damnation if they do not obey acknowledged leaders or other authority figures. At the age of twenty-two, my husband and I faced a situation similar to this. We had moved 1,000 miles from our Midwest homes while I attended graduate school in Alabama. Among our neighbors, Steve and I were considered outsiders, "Northerners" with strange accents and different mores. We felt intensely isolated and homesick for our geographical roots in the Midwest.

Steve and I began attending a small charismatic church, an informal Bible fellowship that included people I had met while visiting the university for an interview the previous spring. Church members initially appeared highly committed to Christ, deeply supportive of us, and very welcoming. That combination of qualities was just what Steve and I needed to begin developing connections to a community of faith in such a new environment. We quickly became involved in Sunday worship as well as weekday events.

In June of 1975, Steve and I returned to our homes in Indiana and Illinois to prepare for our wedding. A month later, we returned to Alabama as newlyweds. During our absence, the small house church that we had previously attended had merged with another house church in the area. New leadership had arisen, and a strict system of mutual accountability had been put in place.

The congregation of forty to fifty people was divided into several shepherding groups of eight to ten members each. A male leader or "shepherd" was assigned oversight of each group. According to the church's policy and theology, each "shepherd" was literally responsible for the souls, or salvation, of his tiny flock. Hebrews 13:17 was used to justify the intensity of spiritual oversight and direction given. The text states: "Obey your leaders and follow their orders. They watch over your souls without resting, since they must give to God an account of their service. If you obey them, they will do their work gladly; if not, they will do it with sadness, and that would be of no help to you."

The shepherds told members of the fellowship who could visit them and when, what books they were to read about spiritual growth, and what restrictions leadership imposed on how people spent their sabbath day of rest. Those who did not comply were reprimanded for their disobedience. It was frightening to us to see what had become of this once joyful, spontaneous, and close-knit fellowship group in such a short time.

My husband and I were given numerous teaching tapes to study. Even though Steve had felt a call to the ministry since high school and had deferred his seminary training while I finished my graduate degree, he was told by the church elders that God was not sending anyone to seminary. Roger, the head elder, firmly believed that theological education was a corrupting influence of the devil. According to Roger, seminaries were educating people *about God* rather than developing followers *of God*. Years earlier, Roger had considered attending seminary himself. He eventually concluded that God did not want him to go. Thus, he discouraged anyone else from pursuing a seminary degree as well. His feelings about this were so strong that he, in fact, forbade Steve to act on his calling to the ministry.

Steve and I were urged to commit the rest of our lives to this faith community in Alabama. All the other members of the house church had agreed to do this. No one was permitted to leave the group unless that individual or couple was "sent out" by the group itself to begin a new ministry elsewhere.

Steve and I were virtually alone in our misgivings about these directives. We had never felt truly at home in Alabama, nor did we ever have any direct reassurance from God that our membership in this fellowship group was meant to be permanent. We struggled for weeks with the convictions exhibited among this group of professing Christians. Even as we prayed and sought guidance from God, we remained unconvinced that the Holy One was leading us in the directions that the leaders of this house church believed were right for us.

With many mixed feelings, Steve and I decided that we could no longer remain part of this community of faith. It was tremendously difficult to cut ties with those who had welcomed and nurtured us so graciously the previous year when we were newcomers to the area. Steve met with the male elders to announce our decision to leave. Their parting words were unforgettable: "Your blood is on your own head. Your salvation is in danger. We wash our hands of you." With this warning and curse laid upon us, we left.

This was an incredibly painful experience. We were twenty-two-year-old newlyweds who had been married about six weeks when this rupture occurred. It would have been easy to leave the church in bitterness. Rather than give up, we struggled to find a different faith community where we could grow during our remaining ten months in Alabama.

Many people going through these kinds of experiences do, in fact, become dechurched. While Steve and I did not lose our faith or leave the church, we left the charismatic movement that had deeply nurtured us throughout college and during my first year of graduate school. Like many departures among the dechurched, this was an abrupt and painful leave-taking that never offered closure around the issues that divided us or on the questions that we raised.

+ + +

When caught in the grips of religious organizations that use manipulation to control their members, individuals may easily lose their own powers of discernment. A tragic loss of faith often results when, or if, such a person eventually recognizes the abuse taking place or a family member forces the person to leave the group.

Mark was a college student who became a Christian during the early 1980s. As time passed, he grew heavily involved in a Christian group with cultlike tendencies. Mark's passion for following Christ quickly became entangled in a total commitment to this fellowship. In obedience to the teachings of the group, Mark cut off all contact with his biological family. In desperation, his parents hired a deprogrammer to locate Mark and challenge his ideas. The young man eventually renounced his affiliation to the group, yet he missed the intense fervor and unquestioned belief system that this group had offered. As time passed, Mark found himself unable to separate his initial commitment to Christ from his experience within this tight community of followers. Mark became an atheist who shunned all contact with Christians. To him, Christianity became a painful reminder of a confusing, even devastating, experience.

+ + +

Spiritual abuse, whether personal or systemic, is not always overt. At times it occurs unintentionally as a result of insensitive responses and simplistic answers. Individuals who are fragile and hurt are particularly vulnerable to this kind of abuse. Such people hunger for a compassionate and supportive presence. Instead, friends and neighbors may offer either condemnation, which isolates and shames them, or trite theological formulas devoid of substance. Job, the ancient suffering saint who lost children, property, employees, and even his own health in tragedy after tragedy, faced this kind of dilemma.

At first Job's friends came to him, sharing his pain in communal silence as they tossed ashes of mourning and rent their garments in rituals of grief (Job 2:12–13). However, as Job's crisis continued without resolution, his friends became impatient. They began spouting off their personal theories about Job's suffering and began dissecting his relationship with God. In a short time, Job's friends became obstacles to his healing rather than vehicles of God's grace. Throughout Job's long ordeal, he uttered many words of self-defense along with the startling confession, "In trouble like this I need loyal friends—whether I've forsaken God or not" (Job 6:14). What Job's friends provided may have been well-intentioned, but for Job it led to greater misunderstanding and alienation from God. Christians must guard themselves against abusing the wounded under a guise of helpfulness.

+ + +

Dick was depressed. He had worked in the local manufacturing plant for thirty-five years. It closed when Dick was just a few years away from retirement. Since then, life hadn't been going well for Dick. No matter how hard he tried and how much he prayed, nothing seemed to change for long.

Dick knew it would be hard to find other work since his skills were limited, but he never expected it to be as hard as it had been. His wife, Pat, suffered from chronic, gradually worsening health problems. She couldn't manage full-time work even if she found it. Purchasing affordable health coverage was impossible. The financial pressures mounted daily.

Each job that Dick secured turned out to be temporary. He would work for a few months, and then—boom!—there would be more layoffs, his position would disappear, or he just wouldn't be needed anymore. At one time Dick felt confident in his ability to learn new skills and relate to all kinds of people. After three years without steady work, however, Dick was beginning to question his own capabilities.

The folks at church weren't much help. With the first new job or two, they were very encouraging. "God has answered your prayers, Dick, and provided that position just for you!" they exclaimed. "Praise the Lord! We knew that if you waited for God, everything would fall into place, and God would bless you once again, this time even more than at first. When we are faithful through times of testing, that's the way our abundant God works," they proclaimed.

It all seemed to be true, until Dick lost the second job, and the third, and the fourth. After three years he was tired of these comments. Spiritual formulas rang hollow in his ears. His wife had just faced another outpatient procedure that increased the medical debt once again. The threat of losing their house loomed before them. Dick had waited on the Lord. He had prayed. He had been faithful. What was happening? The time of testing had been far too long, and people around Dick were weary of his complaints.

Dick decided it was time to keep his feelings to himself. His anger quickly distilled into a serious depression. Dick came to church every Sunday and wondered why he was there. What could he possibly get out of church? No one seemed to understand what he was facing. No one really had any answers, but the church folks kept spewing them out, even after they had become stale and unhelpful. "It must make them feel better to have something to say to me," Dick reasoned, "but I'd rather have them say nothing or just be there with me than try to explain what is happening to me when it makes no sense. How do they know what I'm feeling? How can anyone know?"

Dick's experience is all too familiar within the church. Long-term crises often defy the simplistic answers of the faithful. It is much easier to support a person in a short-term crisis when casseroles, occasional house calls, and a kind word are needed than it is to walk with another through a long-term crisis that seems to escalate rather than resolve itself as time passes. The temptation to respond like Job's friends did with a series of platitudes and theories about God is ever present. Yet rather than help, such actions usually hinder the healing process in suffering individuals and drive them farther from the God they struggle to follow.

Persons in distress need the compassion and sensitive understanding of those around them, not the pat answers of a faith that doesn't always fit the formulas we create. Sometimes Christians must simply be still and quietly present. They must gently accompany their friends and fellow church members on their journeys of faith, which may be characterized by long periods of protracted suffering. Otherwise, people like Dick often leave the church in disillusionment and distress, feeling that they are truly alone as they face the silence of God and the pain of their situation.

CHAPTER 5

Trapped in
Dysfunctional Systems

Persons dechurched through abuse at the hands of Christian institutions or professing believers often experience four "rules" of the dysfunctional family, whether in their church families, denominations, or families of origin. These four rules—don't think, don't feel, don't talk, and don't trust—are subtle messages designed to silence the individual in question. I heard them mentioned years ago at a conference on Christian Recovery Ministries, and they stuck with me. Donald E. Sloat unpacks them in his book, *Growing up Holy and Wholly: Understanding and Hope For Adult Children of Evangelicals* (Wolgemuth & Hyatt, 1990). Indeed, these powerful messages can be enforced in a variety of ways.

Don't Think

The admonition *Don't think* stifles a child's development of original and independent thought apart from the thoughts of adult authority figures in his or her life. Judgments, ideas, and questions are buried deep within the self unless these views agree with those of the dominant adult. The child learns to placate authority by avoiding conflict.

For a while, this pattern enhances feelings of personal safety; in fact, it is deceptive. The game plan becomes one of keeping the peace at any price. A child who masters the don't think rule develops a facility in conforming outwardly to the ideas and opinions of others while repressing his or her genuine thoughts. Thus, the child never fully experiences the true self. Instead, the "split self" becomes the norm, with one set of thoughts being hidden from public view and another more accepted perspective being presented to others.

Jill's father, Buck, always had the last word in the family. Her mother, Ellen, was a quiet woman who consistently deferred to her husband in matters of discipline and decision making. Throughout Jill's childhood, her father's opinions were unquestioned and uncontested. Even when others disagreed with him, they never did so outwardly. They wouldn't dare, for if they did, Buck would give them a long lecture about why they were mistaken. Like her mother, Jill learned to keep her thoughts to herself.

Jill's younger brother, Mick, became very rebellious as an adolescent. He frequently engaged in shouting matches with Buck that usually ended with Mick being sent to his room for the rest of the night. Sometimes they stopped when Mick was spanked, slapped, or whipped. Jill had no interest in experiencing this kind of conflict herself so she managed to stay out of the way whenever Mick and her father got into arguments. Jill's bedroom became her hiding place.

In young adulthood, Jill discovered that she had a problem in expressing her own ideas. Whenever she got into a conversation about any controversial issue—abortion, taxes, even a conflict at work—she would simply close down. She would become frightened and want to run away. She wasn't about to act on such feelings in adult company, so she would just stand still, frozen and impassive, incapable of expressing her own thoughts.

Spiritually, Jill bounced from one style of Christianity to another depending on what type of church she attended. Every time she read a Christian book of any sort, she would become introspective and fearful that she wasn't spiritual enough. She never questioned anything she read and possessed few skills of spiritual discernment.

Several times when she found herself alone in public places, strangers tried to recruit her for groups with reputations of being cults. She wondered if she looked particularly gullible or vulnerable.

It wasn't until Jill read some comments in a self-help book that she began to clarify what was happening within her. The author identified the characteristics of intellectual abuse, describing it as a type of control over a child's thoughts and ideas that leads the child to suppress his or her own thinking within the family of origin. At last Jill had found a name for what she was experiencing. All those years of placating her father, listening to his ideas while withholding hers, had led Jill to a place where she felt no safety in even having ideas of her own.

Jill eventually sought counseling. After several weeks, the counselor asked Jill one day, "What shall we focus on next week?" Jill decided she wanted to begin learning to say what she was thinking in situations where controversy, conflict, or disagreement occurred. The counselor encouraged her to write the affirmation "I can think for myself" on a note card and carry it around for a week.

The impact of this simple exercise was enormous. For twenty-eight years, Jill had never felt comfortable thinking her own thoughts, sharing her own ideas, and holding her own opinions. She was beginning to discover a whole part of herself that had remained in the shadows her entire life. The possibilities for growth seemed overwhelming, but Jill was no longer content simply listening to others speak without discovering her own voice.

The don't think rule impacts the dechurched in a variety of ways. Some people are haunted by threats of damnation for leaving behind a faith that they once embraced. They are discouraged from thinking about and questioning the beliefs that they were taught to accept. The don't think rule prevents those who have been abused within the church from reflecting on the dynamics of their situation. It also plays itself out among the dechurched if they begin exploring their past but are too frightened to acknowledge their own thoughts about their prior experiences of faith.

Don't Feel

While the don't think rule leads to a split between thinking and affirming one's genuine thoughts, the *don't feel* rule creates a split between good and bad emotions. The good emotions are exemplified by qualities such as happiness, kindness, self-sacrifice, gentleness, and joy. The bad emotions are represented by feelings such as anger, bitterness, depression, shame, guilt, and pain. Anger is treated as particularly inappropriate, especially when it is directed toward authority figures in one's life. Legitimate anger about abuse is repressed. The abuser encourages the abused to respond with either silence or shallow acts of forgiveness.

The don't feel rule disallows the reality of struggle within the Christian experience. Continual victory over all negative feelings is expected, and at times is even demanded, as a sign of godliness. Anything less than victory is viewed as wallowing in sin and rebellion. When feelings that are deemed unacceptable are repressed, they easily become objects of shame and guilt. This cycle of denial quickly spirals into symptoms of depression, inappropriate behavior, or ill health.

Scripture verses are often used to buttress this insistence on expressing only positive feelings. "We know that in all things God works for good with those who love him, those whom he has called according to his purpose" (Romans 8:28) is quoted to mean that God is to be praised for everything, no matter how wrong or tragic. Yet this verse does not say that *all things are good*. It merely testifies to the fact that God can redeem even the worst sorrows, tragedies, or abuse in the lives of believers. Such hardships may cripple us, but they need not utterly destroy us. To disallow the reality of human pain and grief is a grave mistake that only pits our feelings against our faith. Instead, God would have us struggle with our feelings, identify the sources of our injuries, and process what happens in our lives honestly in the light of divine love, mercy, justice, and grace.

It is not enough for Christians to strive toward moral honesty. We also must seek to become emotionally honest people. It is only by acknowledging our most difficult emotions that we own them, understand them, and experience their transformation. Our feelings, both good and bad, are a gift from God. They help us to know ourselves. They help us to understand our pain as well as our potential. An acceptance of our feelings is necessary if we are ever to begin repairing the split self.

For years in my own life, I had no healthy outlet for expressing anger. When I got angry as a child, I was quickly overwhelmed with shame and remorse. Sometimes, I took my anger out on myself. Instead of addressing an external problem, miscommunication, or injury directly, I brooded on the problem, turning my feelings inward. Before long I concluded that *I* was the problem. Regularly internalized, my anger gradually distilled into self-loathing and depression. I constantly accepted the responsibility for conflicts around me whether I was at fault or not. I often blamed myself for situations that were beyond my control. I smoothed over hurts and minimized their intensity when confronted by the very people who hurt me.

As I began to see the unhealthy patterns rooted in the don't feel rule, I developed the capacity, little by little, to begin changing them. The transformation of this rule only occurs when we allow ourselves to feel all that we feel, yet are willing to accept full responsibility for dealing with our feelings in appropriate ways. It is not appropriate to feel angry toward someone and go hurt that person in retaliation. Neither is it appropriate to feel angry with someone and proceed to hurt ourselves. There are healthy ways to deal with conflict, injury, and distress.

Those who live by the don't feel rule are often conditioned to ignore their deepest reactions and sorrows. They have buried the experiences that evoke these strong feelings deep in their hearts for no one to see, even themselves. One of the real challenges of ministry among the dechurched is reaching into another's life over time in such a way that the don't feel rule is challenged and begins losing its power.

Don't Talk

The third rule, *don't talk,* emphasizes loyalty over truthful dialogue. That loyalty may be to a church family, cultlike group, parent, boss, or any other authority figure. Questioning authority is forbidden. Frequently, an us-against-them mentality enhances the isolation of the group from others who would break the silence.

When Josie began to explore the don't talk rule in her family, she realized that it went back at least three generations. Josie grew up in a church-going family that didn't talk much about religion at home. As a young adult, she was invited to attend a vibrant Bible study group. It was there that Josie made a personal commitment to follow Jesus Christ.

When Josie was in her twenties, she began exploring the dynamics within her family of origin. Two of her aunts were thoroughly dechurched. Her grandmother had been a devout, yet demanding, Christian. Josie occasionally overheard rumors that Grandma had suffered from emotional instability that brought on bouts of rage. Grandma was an extremely harsh disciplinarian.

No one ever really talked about Grandma's difficult temperament and its toll on the family. No one ever shared with another in a way that led them to explore their own feelings about the inconsistencies between Grandma's public faith and the way she treated her children privately. Josie always wondered if Grandma's practice of Christianity was at the root of her two aunts' adverse reactions to the faith, but she could never get them to discuss religion. The topic was "off limits." Everyone else in the family—except Josie—just accepted that.

One day Josie got her mother talking about the silence that the family maintained regarding Grandma's faith and violent outbursts. It was a touchy subject, and Josie knew it, but she felt compelled to search for answers to her questions about her own family history. Her mother began by quoting the scripture, "Respect your father and your mother, so that you may live a long time in the land that I am giving you" (Exodus 20:12). She nearly whispered to her daughter, "Every time any of us wanted to question what was happening at home, your grandmother used this scripture to elicit our unquestioning obedience. She reminded us that our place as children was to honor our parents and acknowledge them as God's instruments for our own good. To this day that scripture stands as a monument to my parents' expectations for us as children."

Josie began realizing that this verse in Exodus had been used to maintain two subsequent generations of silence about her grandmother's unresolved personal problems. Secretly, she wondered if her grandma had struggled with some sort of mental illness, as the woman seemed given to bouts of depression and fits of intense activity. Josie had read enough in textbooks and magazines to recognize the symptoms of mental illness. She was convinced that untreated mental illness could deeply impact a person's expression of faith. Yet mental illness was another topic that was off limits within the family system. Even if it existed and was acknowledged, mental illness would be considered a shameful family secret, not an actual physiological condition for which help was available.

Josie wished that someone would confront the impact of her grandmother's behavior within the family system. She recognized the effects of Grandma's patterns into her mother's generation and even into her own. No one ever tackled this issue except Josie. She was determined to break the don't talk rule in her own generation. To do that, she had to grapple with the silence that had impacted her family system and how it had affected her as a young adult.

+ + +

David was barely out of his teens and, ironically, was already dechurched when I first met him. *How could that be?* I wondered to myself. *He is so young and has so much of life ahead of him,* I mused. What I found was that David did not grow up in the church, but became a Christian through the witness of neighbors as a child. He had immersed himself in the life of the church for several years. I asked him why he left. "I still had lots of questions about Christianity after I was saved," David said. "I tried to ask them, but no one wanted to listen. People quoted the scripture in James that says, 'Whoever doubts is like a wave in the sea that is driven and blown about by the wind. A person like that, unable to make up his mind and undecided in all he does, must not think that he will receive anything from the Lord' (James 1:6b–8). They told me to just trust the Lord, and everything would make sense. I needed to struggle with my questions of faith and doubt, but I just couldn't do it in the church, so I left."

+ + +

The don't talk rule is toxic within the church and home, the workplace or mission organization. It stifles the very honesty that is required to tackle difficult issues and forge ahead with significant growth. It leaves people stranded, alone with their own questions and convictions, while others choose not to engage themselves in forthright dialogue. Where the don't talk rule is actively enforced, the whistle-blower tragically becomes the outcast. The dechurched must work through the implications of the don't talk rule as it plays itself out in their lives. At times they are eager to speak to anyone who will listen. Often they are too bitter to care.

Don't Trust

Finally, the *don't trust* rule becomes the undergirding reality in any dysfunctional system. Those who learn not to trust as children spend many years unlearning these patterns as adults. There is no easy transition between practicing the don't trust rule and learning to place a firm and full trust in God. Making an ongoing commitment to a church or Christian fellowship becomes an even more difficult challenge. Frequently, those with impaired abilities to trust are susceptible to placing their trust in unhealthy institutions or individuals and getting hurt all over again.

The issue of trust comes up repeatedly in the ministry that my husband and I share. Years ago, I led a Bible study group for women, many of whom had been dechurched at one point or another in their lives. Nearly everybody in the group was struggling with some major difficulty. One battled episodic mental illness that was utterly debilitating for extended periods of time. Another was a survivor of sexual abuse. Her tough exterior masked deep feelings of shame and unworthiness. One woman suffered from fractured family relationships beginning when she married a man her parents disliked. Still another was in counseling for symptoms of clinical depression.

Throughout the weekly Bible study, none of these women ever shared even a sliver of their personal struggles with the others present. The prayers they offered bore none of the authentic angst and struggle of their real lives. Prayer times were filled with wonderful platitudes about God and general requests for the healing of others but never mentioned the incredible obstacles these women themselves were facing. The Bible study was textually nuanced and academically rigorous. Group members regularly highlighted additional texts that related to the topic. Thoughtful questions about interpretation and context were raised. I sensed that the women were determined to focus on the meaning of each biblical text but never on the meaning of their own lives.

I hated watching this happen. I realized the superficiality of this experience because individuals had shared their private agonies with me at one time or another. I ached to see just a glimmer of honesty, authenticity, and soul-baring occur among these hurting women. I yearned to gaze on tears streaming down flushed cheeks. Even shouts and loud sobs would have been cleansing experiences for some in the group. None of these events took place. When the study ended after twelve weeks, everyone quietly returned to their own pain and thanked me for leading such valuable group discussions. I could barely stand it.

The experience, however, brought home to me the intensity of the don't trust rule as it operates in the lives of the formerly dechurched. Is the Christian community a safe place to trust others with secrets of mental illness, sexual abuse, or marital distress? The church had not provided such a refuge for these people in the past. Even in a new environment where questions were valued, struggles accepted, and defeats acknowledged, how could these women know if another group member was trustworthy or might turn against them at a time when they least expected it?

Many times the dechurched have been horribly betrayed by Christian friends, churches, or family members. Sometimes the church has prematurely given up on a person who needed support rather than rebuke or a listening ear rather than a lecture. It is not easy for the one who has been deeply hurt to open up again. Gaining the trust of the dechurched who have been schooled in the don't trust rule is a slow process. It invariably includes many setbacks along the way. Developing an awareness of this rule is a first step toward reopening a wounded heart.

+ + +

Don't think. Don't feel. Don't talk. Don't trust. These four rules of the dysfunctional system are often deeply embedded in the lives of those dechurched by abuse. The journey toward wholeness is not quick nor easy. Patterns that took years to develop ultimately can take years to overcome. Jesus reminds us, "In the world ye shall have tribulation: but be of good cheer; I have overcome the world" (John 16:33b, KJV). The journey is hard, but it is good.

CHAPTER 6

Paralyzed by Trauma

While many dechurched people have experienced abuse at the hands of churches or professing Christians, others face trauma that is never adequately processed on a spiritual level. Tragedies are frequently inexplicable; they strike when we least expect them. They can shatter whatever external sense of security or predictability we feel in life. Trauma visits humanity in a variety of guises—from the terrors of war, famine, and natural disaster to the isolated acts of violence that arise from carjackings, rapes, or sudden death. For a child, trauma can be as simple as the loss of a beloved pet in spite of the child's anguished prayers. Trauma can also be as complicated as the random murder of a loved one or the unanticipated dissolution of a long marriage.

Trauma comes in three forms. It can be *direct,* a disaster that happens to the self. A car accident may cause several broken bones, or a diving accident may lead to lifelong paralysis. Life as the individual has known it completely stops. A new series of challenges becomes reality, at times for a season or perhaps forever. A serious illness may impact one's activities and opportunities. New limitations creep into one's existence and must be faced on a daily basis. A mugging may escalate one's fear of being alone. Experiences once natural and taken for granted become terrifying obstacles to navigate in wholly unfamiliar ways.

Trauma can also be *indirect,* affecting a person profoundly, yet vicariously. A sibling may be diagnosed with a rare disease. Life for everyone in the family changes dramatically to accommodate the challenges facing the child. A parent may be battered by a spouse while a young child cowers in his bedroom, listening to the shouting and waiting for the cycle of violence to pass.

As trauma directly impacts those around us, we discover that we too are traumatized by these tragedies. We try to make sense of another's pain and find ways to deal with these experiences in light of our own belief systems. The observer of trauma often feels helpless to intervene. Sometimes this person erroneously internalizes blame for the situation at hand.

Indirect trauma can be as devastating as direct trauma. Too frequently, however, the focus remains solely on the survivor of the car accident, the battered spouse, or the terminally ill patient. Attention must also be given to those silent, suffering survivors affected by the trauma their loved ones face. The silent pain felt by the witness to trauma is often experienced as if the tragedy were in fact one's own.

+ + +

Juan and Ramona began attending church after being dechurched for several years. Both had spent their late teens living wildly and giving little thought to the consequences of their behaviors. In their early twenties they met and married, continuing their lifestyle of partying and substance abuse. One day they attended a mass evangelism rally at the invitation of a friend. Deeply moved, they both walked up to the altar and made a commitment to Christ.

Juan and Ramona took this new commitment very seriously. They made profound adjustments in their lifestyle as they sought to follow Christ. They raised the children they subsequently bore within the Christian faith. They tended to be loners, however, and rarely engaged the wider Christian community. They gradually developed their own "homegrown" approach to Christianity.

One day, Juan and Ramona were invited by neighbors to attend a local church. The pastor, Ray, began reaching out to them. Within a few months, Juan and Ramona joined the church. While participation in a community of faith was new for them, they enjoyed the people at the church and began making new friends. They became very close to the pastor's family.

Unexpectedly, Ramona called Pastor Ray in a panic. That morning, amid an argument with Ramona, Juan had threatened to kill himself and their two small children. He had experienced periods of depression characterized by withdrawal and stony silence in the past, but he had never talked like this. Ramona was terrified. She did not know where Juan was, but she worried about the safety of herself and the children. Pastor Ray encouraged her to find safe shelter away from her home and then spent his day trying to track down Juan.

When Juan was finally located, he had calmed down quite a bit and was willing to talk with Pastor Ray. As the conversation unfolded, Pastor Ray became convinced that Juan needed more specialized help than he could offer. Ray called an area counselor who was willing to see Juan immediately to evaluate his condition and long-term needs. Juan was surprisingly receptive to this idea and began seeing the counselor on a regular basis.

As the months of therapy unfolded, it became clear that Juan's father had frequently beaten his wife during alcoholic binges and that, for years, Juan silently observed these episodes. Even as a child, he suffered incredible guilt and remorse that he had done nothing to stop this abuse. By the time Juan reached adulthood, these feelings of self-blame distilled into a deep depression occasionally broken by outbursts of rage.

The shame and guilt that Juan had carried since his boyhood was killing him. In fact, it was this pent-up rage that had led to the explosive incident with his wife and children. Juan's long struggle with clinical depression and its causes had gone unattended for a lifetime. Several years of counseling and support helped Juan process these horrible experiences and eventually forgive himself for not protecting his mother. Juan experienced indirect trauma that affected every day of his life.

+ + +

Trauma can also be *insidious,* or societal in its impact. Examples include the effects of racism or war. Natural disasters are also insidious traumas that indiscriminately impact large numbers of people over wide geographical areas. Such experiences are invasive and impossible to address on a solely personal level. Even when the trauma is shared with others within a larger group, the long-term effects of insidious trauma can wear down individuals or entire populations in ways that make them feel isolated, forsaken, and disheartened.

Throughout the history of the church, the linkage of Christianity with racism has led to people's becoming dechurched. Sam, an African American campus minister, reflects on questions he hears from African American college students. "How can I justify being a Christian when Christians have historically supported slavery and segregation? How can some organizations call themselves 'Christian' yet preach hatred and the racial supremacy of white people? What kind of Christ is this?"

Sam worries about the number of college students he meets who feel they cannot struggle with their questions of faith, ethnicity, and justice within the church. When they ask serious questions or express sincere doubts, many are told by their pastors and friends that questioning the authority of scripture or Christian doctrine is wrong. Within the faith community, they are not offered adequate opportunities to wrestle with the many ideas that bombard them from all sides in the classroom and on campus. "Too many young African American students are simply leaving the church to explore their questions elsewhere. What a great tragedy this is for the church," Sam comments.

Racism remains an insidious presence in the contemporary church. The church's long history of complicity with racism is well-documented and undeniable. It does the institution of the church no good to deny this history, minimize it, or insist that the problem was solved decades ago by changes in national laws. Racism encompasses more than individual acts of discrimination; it also grows within structural patterns that enhance the privileges of some while disenfranchising others.

The dechurched who have borne the brunt of racism both in the histories of their people and their own experiences ask tough and serious questions of the church. It is not enough for Christians to merely address individual acts of prejudice. The church must also be prepared to tackle the larger picture, take responsibility for its sins, and work for justice.

Interfaith tensions also exist as individuals exit the church and turn to other faiths. According to media reports, one inner-city dialogue between black pastors and area leaders within the Nation of Islam turned ugly with shouting matches between attendees and a walkout among some clergy. At issue was the increase of African American males embracing the tenets of the Nation of Islam rather than Christianity. Charges and countercharges were leveled about the effectiveness of different religious groups as they reached out to the most vulnerable and at-risk youth on the city streets. While the topic was obviously an extremely sensitive one to both sides of the debate, it raised deep questions for the church about the dechurched beyond its doors. Who reaches out to them? How is the church fulfilling its calling in society? What happens to those who cannot find what they seek within the church or who never make it into our buildings?

As a white woman, I certainly cannot begin to speak adequately about complex social and contextual realities that face varied races and socially marginalized groups as they struggle to address the needs of the dechurched in their midst. Within each unique ministry context around the country and even throughout the world, there is challenging and creative work to be done. Regardless of our skin color or ethnicity, as Christians we must face the issues we would rather not address, ask the questions we cannot always clearly answer, and listen to the voices that are most difficult for us to hear.

A missionary from a poor nation in Central America shared his observations of the many divisions that occurred between congregations during his term of service. Political infighting and theological differences, as well as exhaustion from a protracted civil war, took their toll on many churches. The religious landscape was littered with the dechurched.

The problems we face with insidious trauma reach far beyond our neighborhoods and congregations. It is imperative that the church offer the dechurched more than a simple message about personal piety, which alone is vitally important, but will not be completely sufficient in addressing the needs of this population.

The church must also open its eyes to the social influences that impact individuals, neighborhoods, and even nations. Such realities affect our ability to renew our vision for the coming reign of God and to work on its behalf.

Fears that surround cultural and racial differences can provoke insidious trauma. Fear of disintegrating traditional sexual mores can also reach a fever pitch of hysteria and inflict serious damage in the lives of individuals who have trusted the church to provide love and support. Such was the case for Sally.

+ + +

Sally was a seminary student completing a degree in pastoral counseling. Her family owned several pets when she was a child, and she had always loved working with animals. As Sally completed her field ministry assignment in an institution for the elderly and mentally disabled persons, she struggled with the conditions of her patients. She realized that many had withdrawn long ago from the affections of other humans. Sally began wondering if they would respond to well-trained house pets. She spoke with her supervisors and was given permission to design a "pet ministry" as part of her field training.

It wasn't long before Sally noticed hints of smiles on the faces of her formerly impassive patients. Flora, who usually repelled human touch, awkwardly reached down and patted the head of a friendly dog. Floyd chuckled quietly as a furry little kitten curled up in his lap. Sally was overjoyed and deeply touched that her vision of reaching patients through animals was proving to be successful.

Sally shared her enthusiasm about her work with those in her church. They disliked the concept of a pet ministry and considered it "weird." Rumors began flying. Before long, Sally was brought before the elders of the church on charges of bestiality. She was shocked and appalled. Sally had been part of the church all her life. How could these friends and mentors suspect that she could ever commit such acts? Sally's decision to use animals in her ministry had been prompted by her love for God and her care for the broken in spirit.

Sally was devastated. The church leaders urged her to repent and return to Christ. She proclaimed her innocence again and again, but even as she did so, she realized that she had little hope of convincing the church elders. They were sure she was guilty. They told Sally that she could either repent or renounce all ties to this church of her childhood. The stakes grew higher and higher. Sally could not imagine being cast out of the church she loved, nor could she imagine confessing what she did not do. She faced unremitting pressure to admit her guilt.

When Sally came to me, she felt angry, confused, and betrayed. She realized that there was no turning back. She would never again be able to have the relationship with her church that she once took for granted. Nor could she ever share the joys of her ministry with these church folk who did not trust anything as unusual to them as a "pet ministry." Sally had stopped going to church anywhere, but she was aching for the fellowship that had been so important to her for most of her life.

What should Sally have done? I counseled her to make a fresh start. I encouraged her to look around for a new community of faith. I also suggested that she seek counseling in order to work through her grief and feelings of shame over this incident that had driven her from the church. As we continued speaking about the situation, it was clear to me that deep-seated fears of sexual aberration had played themselves out within the congregation and led to their indictment of this young woman. Sally and I began exploring the interfacing of social and congregational fears. We examined her experiences of both direct and insidious trauma.

+ + +

Many times trauma is not adequately processed because an individual's theology prevents the integration of the trauma into his or her life. Those who face the untimely death of a family member may conclude that a loving God would not allow them to experience such pain. They continue reasoning, "If God exists, then God must not be loving. Why follow an unloving God?" Those who do not discover the inner resources necessary to navigate suffering in the light of faith often harbor such lines of thinking.

Claire's story illustrates this struggle. Claire was a college sophomore when her mother died during surgery. The two of them had enjoyed an exceptionally close emotional bond over the years.

Claire was utterly devastated by her mother's death. She had grown up in a middle-class Christian family and had encountered very little adversity in her life. Subconsciously, Claire had always believed that God protected those who lived good lives. She had been taught in the church that God sheltered the faithful from harm. When her mother died, everything changed. Claire had done her part; what about God? Claire felt betrayed, abandoned, and alone. She was furious with God. Her formula for receiving God's blessing had failed. Throughout her childhood, it had remained untested, and when it was finally put to the test, it was found wanting. Claire's understanding of God could not hold up in the face of this unexpected tragedy.

+ + +

Our lives are filled with people like Claire, Sally, and Juan, whose lives have been irrevocably changed by trauma. Their stories may be different, but the themes are similar. Tom's best friend died in a tragic accident thirty-five years ago, and Tom hasn't entered the doors of a church since the funeral. Tina's favorite farm animal was sold at an auction, and no one in the family recognized the young girl's enduring sense of loss. Social rejection wore Andrew down and took its toll as he struggled to reconcile his Christian faith with his sexual orientation. The temptation is great for each person to quietly slip out of the pew, away from the fellowship of others, afraid to tell his or her own story and experience redemption.

CHAPTER 7

Addicted to Religion

While trauma and abuse leave many people dechurched, addiction also creates havoc in an individual's life. Among the dechurched, addiction can cloak itself in a religious guise. The spiritual journey, initially embraced as a liberating experience, becomes a substitute for facing painful realities of childhood and/or adulthood. The individual throws all the passion once reserved for other addictive behaviors into the religious experience. A short-lived period of intense growth and service is marked by obsessive religious activity. As time passes, alienation from family, friends, coworkers, and others results. Before the religious addict stops to look at what is truly happening, his or her life may spin out of control toward some kind of emotional or physical breakdown, a threatened or actual divorce, or a job loss.

+ + +

Valerie's experience with Christianity bore the marks of religious addiction. During her early twenties, she joined a fast-growing, nondenominational congregation. Valerie volunteered to help with nearly every aspect of congregational life. She served on numerous committees and attended the majority of events listed on the church calendar. The day came, however, when the pastor was charged with sexual indiscretions, and Valerie was falsely implicated. Amid a swirl of allegations and counterallegations, the pastor found ways to shore up his own support while Valerie was shunned by the congregation she had so faithfully served.

Valerie left the church, wounded and shamed. She began volunteering at a battered women's shelter. There Valerie was shocked to discover the number of abused women who came from supposedly Christian homes. Their stories all sounded alike. Years of abuse followed one another as these women worked hard to become better wives and accept full responsibility for their predicaments. They heeded the advice of pastors who blamed them, rather than their abusive spouses, for the violence that they faced. "Stay home, pray, submit to your husband, and God will bless you," one pastor counseled. Another admonished his parishioner, "Search your heart for the disobedience that is causing your husband to harm you."

Experiences such as these forced Valerie to reexamine issues of power, sexuality, and Christian spirituality. She began to make connections between her own experiences within the church and some of the patterns of adaptation that these battered women had developed over the years in order to survive. Valerie discovered that her total immersion in serving others had masked many critical areas of faith development that she had consistently neglected.

The longer Valerie explored the dynamics of spousal abuse, the more she began recognizing unhealthy relationships in her own life. Why did she gravitate toward powerful people, on one hand, or extremely needy people, on the other? Why did she so often find herself getting used by the very people she utterly trusted?

Valerie stopped running from the many unresolved issues of her past and began confronting them, one by one. She reexamined beliefs that she had once accepted without question. She reconsidered the ways that Christian theology had been used to reinforce violence against the residents at the battered women's shelter. She was furious with the pastors who had ignored, rather than confronted, the culpability of the abusers.

Valerie still believed that there was hope for the church. She sought and found a new church home that she hoped would be more open to her emerging sensitivities and concerns. After attending services for several months, Valerie began speaking out about the plight of battered Christian women. She quickly discovered that her insights and critiques were unwelcome. Some church members considered Valerie's questions and observations inappropriate or even heretical. It wasn't long before Valerie realized that she was no longer welcome there.

In an attempt to find a place where issues of gender, power, sexuality, and faith were openly discussed, Valerie visited several other churches. Remaining in church became more and more difficult for her as she faced silence and denial wherever she went. Eventually, Valerie abandoned the church in pursuit of a woman-centered spirituality more sensitive to the issues facing abused women. Tragically, the churches she attended neglected to engage the spiritual and moral issues of critical importance to Valerie while she was still searching for a deeper Christian faith.

+ + +

Barbara grew up in a Jewish family that did not observe or teach the rituals of the Jewish faith. At the age of twenty-seven she converted to Christianity. At the urging of Christian neighbors, she joined a local congregation. Throughout most of her life, Barbara had never thought much about spiritual matters, yet she was drawn to the faith that her neighbors embraced. She openly shared the fact that she was Jewish but had not been raised as a practicing Jew.

Within a few months after Barbara's "conversion," she became the showcase of attention within the church. She was the "Jewish Christian" among them and was thrust into the limelight to provide public testimonials about her conversion experience. The longer Barbara continued within the church, the more she began wondering about the meaning of her Jewish heritage. However, she felt that she dare not discuss her questions among her newfound Christian friends.

One day Barbara decided to visit a synagogue located in the large suburban community where she resided. As she listened to the scripture readings recited in Hebrew and observed the rituals she had never learned in her family of origin, Barbara began to sense an incredible homecoming within the deepest parts of herself. Persistent questions nibbling around the corners of her mind quickly became a floodgate for surging thoughts and feelings. "Why have I known so little about my past? What was the history of my parents and their parents before them?" she wondered.

Barbara began attending the synagogue more often and the church less frequently. Her Christian friends could not understand this about-face. They doubted her sincerity of faith and prayed for her double-mindedness. Before long, Barbara left the Christian fellowship and embraced the Jewish faith. This whole journey, which began with an exploration of Christianity, led Barbara back to her Jewish roots. She was determined to discover who she really was and what her family truly believed.

As Barbara explored her own past as well as that of previous generations, she learned about one relative who had died in the Holocaust, then another, and another. She discovered that a favorite uncle had survived the death camps, but had never spoken to her about his experiences. These terrible secrets remained hidden in the fabric of her family history. Barbara concluded that much of the silenced pain within her family system was rooted in the ways that her family had coped with the terrors of the Holocaust and the shattering of any trust in God that resulted.

Barbara began to interpret her brief experience with Christianity as a part of her continued attempt to skirt the unspoken issues of her family history and personal life. She was raised with no real knowledge of her own heritage as a Jewish woman. Barbara longed to understand the richness and blessing of this promise. "Maybe I will be a Christian again someday," she spoke quietly. "But, whether that happens or not, right now I have to find out who I really am, what the stories of my ancestors really mean for my life, and what issues have profoundly impacted the silences of my childhood. I need to find out what it means for me to be Jewish."

Barbara's brief conversion to Christianity became a catalyst through which she eventually gained deep insights about herself and her family of origin. On the outside, it seemed to the Christians within Barbara's church that she was rejecting the God that they had shared so freely with her. On the inside, Barbara interpreted her Christian experiences as an opportunity to begin exploring her spirituality for the first time. This journey led her into the past to face the "ghosts" that inhabited the closets of her family life.

+ + +

Many times, people who undergo quick conversions later step back to sort out what it is they are seeking. Sometimes their initial embrace of religious faith provides an escape from unresolved personal or family issues. Nelly was such a person. As a child, her family had been very active in a Baptist church, but Nelly hadn't attended any church for several years. I met her at a time when her marriage was falling apart. We quickly developed a friendship around the activities of our children, who were close in age.

Nelly recommitted her life to Christ and joined a women's fellowship group. There she found ongoing support during the rough times in her marriage, which were numerous. Nelly had high hopes for her husband's conversion. She was certain it would turn their relationship around. Every time the women gathered, Nelly prayed for her husband, Bob. Every day, she looked for changes in his behavior. Yet, rather than appreciate Nelly's newfound faith, Bob felt it was an intrusion in their relationship. He seemed more contentious than ever.

Nelly tried all kinds of means, both subtle and overt, to pique Bob's interest in spiritual matters. Nothing worked. She tried being open and welcoming. She tried being dutiful and silent. Either way, her best efforts seemed to be taken for granted. Nelly began to lose interest in Christianity.

As I watched this scenario unfold, I discovered something significant about Nelly that I had not noticed at first. It didn't seem that she was interested in the totality of Christian discipleship. What she wanted from recommitting her life to Christ was a changed marriage. Period. That was it.

In the women's fellowship group, Nelly hardly ever prayed for anything except her family. She rarely talked about her spiritual growth beyond her husband's latest reactions to the changes she was attempting to make in herself. Somehow, Nelly seemed to think that becoming a Christian would provide a surefire transformation of her marriage. When tensions between Nelly and Bob mounted instead of easing, Nelly questioned the existence of God.

Nelly had many personal issues to confront in order to genuinely follow Christ. The first of these was to decide whether she was truly interested in a life of Christian discipleship or just a quick fix for her troubled marriage.

+ + +

Religious addiction is characterized by the masking of authentic needs and problems under a veneer of spiritual practice or commitment. Such behavior at times is coupled with intense emotional engagement. Frequently, churches encourage new believers to continually praise the Lord amid all the highs and lows that characterize their lives. While praising God is a precious act of worship, an enforced joy too frequently masks a deeply troubled spirit beneath the surface. That joy can at times obscure serious depression, pain, rage, or even secret sin.

Religious addiction fosters a split life. The outer life may be touched up and polished for the approval of other believers, while the inner life may be tortured and painful, compulsive and driven. The spirit may be anything but free.

In this context God, church, religion, and religious activity can become an escape from reality, a "fix" to make the person feel better. A religious addict may be preaching to everyone nearby, but listening to no one, including his or her own deepest self. The religious addict may be late to a job or chronically neglect family obligations while doing "God's work." A religious addict may quote scripture often, read nothing but religious literature, and attend to nothing but religion while avoiding the profoundly spiritual work of the soul. The addiction can overtake his or her life.

To place Christ first in one's life is the call of the gospel. Yet even amid that call, we must balance the needs of family, work, neighbors, and ourselves. Whenever we use our spirituality to mask the authentic needs and struggles that we face, we are caught *playing* Christian rather than *being* Christian. In this bind, we must stop, identify what we fear, and find a way to discover God's grace in the midst of our pain.

CHAPTER 8

Haunted by Mental Illness

After a workshop I led on ministry among the dechurched, Pastor Will waited to speak with me. Throughout my whirlwind overview of a six-hour workshop presented in an hour and a half, I frequently made eye contact with him. He vigorously nodded his head time and time again as I spoke. He also took notes at a furious pace. Out of the forty people in the room, it seemed that Pastor Will's experience in ministry resonated most deeply with my comments and observations on working among this population. I was glad he stopped to talk with me after I finished. I was curious to learn what ministry he himself had been doing among those who had left the church.

Pastor Will told me about a man named Nick whom he had befriended three years earlier. Nick never talked about his previous experiences in the church. His life seemed to contain some huge secret that defied confession. Finally, one day Nick blurted out his hidden story: "My father was diagnosed with manic depression when I was a child. He had a hard life dealing with his mental illness. Five years ago, he committed suicide."

Within Nick's faith tradition, he and his family understood suicide as a mortal sin for which there was no absolution. Since the time of his father's death, Nick had carried around this terrible tragedy from which he could find no spiritual relief.

Once Nick exposed his secret, he began expressing his yearning to make peace with God over his father's mental illness and subsequent suicide. Nick had not celebrated the eucharist, or Lord's supper, since his father had passed away. Taking communion only reminded him of the agony of his father's life and the unfinished business of his father's death. Nick spent many hours with Pastor Will as they explored the interfacing of mental illness and Christian commitment in the life of Nick's father. Nick wept as he shared his own pain in watching his father struggle, falter, and pick himself up again and again. Nick also faced his anger and grief over the ways his father's illness had impacted his family life over several decades.

Slowly, Nick began to trust himself once more to the God of mercy and grace, the God who loved even Nick's tortured father. One day, Nick returned to church. He celebrated communion for the first time in six years. This act was an important step for Nick in the long, slow healing process taking place deep within his soul.

+ + +

Jana also faced a painful struggle with mental illness in her family. She was one of the quietest college students I have ever met. In group situations, she rarely contributed to the discussion. At church, she sat by herself and left immediately after the service. When she finally came to see me, however, she could barely contain her words.

When Jana was a child, her mother, Marlene, was diagnosed with schizophrenia. Jana's father was passive and withdrawn, letting Marlene set the tone for family interactions. Marlene's instability impacted every member of the household. She developed strict religious expectations for her children. Jana and her siblings were not allowed to eat supper at night without first reciting a list of memorized scriptures. If they repeated the verses incorrectly, the children were sent to their rooms without dinner. Jana recalled her paralyzing fear as she sat before the cooked meal and tried to repeat her Bible verses perfectly.

At age twenty, Jana felt that she believed in God, yet she was very confused about the substance of her faith. The God she experienced as a child was terrifying. The Bible she experienced as a child was overwhelming. The faith she experienced as a child was crippling. Jana had begun professional counseling to make sense of her past. She hoped that I could help her think through the interfacing of her spirituality with the other factors operative at home.

Each week, Jana and I explored various articles that related to issues of the dechurched. She sought to identify the many difficulties that arose whenever mental illness influenced the way a person expressed his or her Christian faith. We talked a great deal about the lack of literature linking these areas. Mental illness and Christian spirituality are often wed in complicated, unhealthy patterns that must be untangled as best they can in order to be named and understood.

+ + +

The church has not done its homework on the impact of untreated mental illness in the practice of Christian faith. Articles written on the topic are hard to find. Christians know how to support a woman struggling with cancer, a man recovering from heart surgery, or the family with a new baby, but mental illness remains a mystery. Periods of dysfunction come and go; the impact of mental illness rises and falls. It can turn a family inside out for years at a time.

Mental illness can lead to long-term crises with no end in sight. Too often, family members trying to piece life together are left to struggle alone. Mental illness can create misunderstandings and silences in the church simply because people do not know how to respond, what to say, or what to do.

Mental illness affects one's spirituality in profound ways that are not easily unraveled. A person with schizophrenia frequently hears voices and sees visions; their senses are heightened. Without medication, paranoia can go unchecked. When the schizophrenic is committed to Christ, he or she frequently cannot distinguish between the voice of God and the voices of schizophrenia. "God told me that you must be punished," or "God told me that you are watching everything I do," may become certainties in the minds of the mentally ill. Friends may deny or repudiate these suspicions or directives, but to no avail. Members of the congregation may also become the objects of paranoia. The health of a church can be adversely impacted by one person's untreated mental illness. The health of a family can be devastated.

+ + +

Ted struggles daily with an obsessive-compulsive disorder. He is unable to separate his psychological handicap from his spirituality. The perfectionism and attention to detail that accompany his illness drive the practice of his faith as well. "Am I OK? Did I do well enough?" become Ted's incessant questions as he rechecks his motives, actions, and even his prayers. Ted latches on to one concern after another, rolling them around in his thoughts endlessly, convinced that nothing he can do will ever truly please God no matter how hard he tries.

Ted is imprisoned by his behavioral disorder. It directly impacts his understanding of what it means to serve and follow Christ. He needs help discerning the impact of his mental disability on his interpretation and practice of the Christian faith. Medication may help soften this struggle. Inadvertently, a church's theology may reinforce Ted's tortured perfectionism if the church offers constant affirmation for servanthood and self-sacrifice without an equal emphasis on personal wholeness and self-care. Ted needs encouragement to accept the fact that all humans are imperfect. He also needs to be warmly and unconditionally embraced as he struggles with his illness.

+ + +

The tragic effects of untreated mental illness in the family can, even unintentionally, lead to abuse in the lives of children. The mentally ill adult or sibling may be well-intentioned yet completely unaware of the impact of the illness on family members. At times the family remains in complete denial that mental illness even exists among its own. A child may carry a deep affection for the affected parent or sibling while simultaneously harboring a simmering rage at the impact of the illness on the family and the self. This conflict must be acknowledged and explored. Distortions of spirituality as manifested through the illness must be confronted, named, and understood as much as possible. Otherwise, the child may face spiritual confusion as the effects of the illness are merged with a crippled understanding of God.

How can I believe again? is perhaps the question asked by survivors of families confronting all types of abuse, trauma, addiction, or mental illness. There is a pathway, but it is not clearly marked. The resources to explore it are few, but the traveling companion is Jesus, and he can lead the way.

CHAPTER 9

Disillusioned by Irrelevancy

Helena described her personal history of being dechurched to me: "I became so disillusioned with the church's lack of relevancy, I just couldn't stay anymore. What eventually led me back to the church was visiting a congregation that was active in the sanctuary movement."

During the 1980s, the sanctuary movement offered a response of conscience and dissent toward U.S. immigration policy regarding refugees from Central America. U.S. policy disallowed the designation of "political refugee" for many who had fled repressive regimes in Latin America that were backed by the United States. Others who fled similarly repressive regimes were welcomed as political refugees if they were fleeing countries considered enemies of the United States. These people could find welcome in the U.S. while others facing war, persecution, and repression could not.

Church groups protested this policy in a variety of ways. The most controversial avenue of dissent was performing acts of civil disobedience and declaring one's church a sanctuary church. Such congregations defied the U.S. policy of denying legal status to political refugees from places such as El Salvador or Guatemala by offering sanctuary, protection, shelter, and resources to these refugees. It was the hope of such churches that the United States government would recognize these acts of civil disobedience as acts of faith and conscience, acts of caring for the neighbor as North Americans wished to be cared for themselves.

Would such a direct challenge from pockets within the religious community lead government leaders toward a rethinking of this refugee policy? Even if it did not, members of sanctuary churches still found comfort in providing safety, care, and ministry to many individuals traumatized by war, kidnappings, and other systemic injustices within their own countries.

Other congregations advocating a change of policy found different ways to support dispossessed refugees who were denied permanent residency in the United States. In Oberlin, churches worked together to form a network called The Overground Railroad. This organization was named after the Underground Railroad that, a century earlier, had harbored escaped slaves on their way to freedom in Canada.

The Overground Railroad became a way station for refugees who applied for political asylum in the United States. Until their applications were denied, such refugees were legally granted temporary residency in the United States. Knowing that the process would be protracted and end in rejection, local church members housed refugees in Oberlin while seeking permanent residency for these people in Canada. Several families and individuals remained in Oberlin for a few weeks to a few months while homes were prepared for them on the other side of our northern border.

Not all churches in the United States supported these acts of conscience by sanctuary churches and citizen groups such as The Overground Railroad. Some churches fervently supported U.S. policies on the status of Central American refugees. Many such churches believed that it was the duty of citizens to support the actions of their government without question. They quoted passages such as Romans 13:1–2: "Everyone must obey state authorities, because no authority exists without God's permission, and the existing authorities have been put there by God. Whoever opposes the existing authority opposes what God has ordered; and anyone who does so will bring judgment on himself."

Civil dissent, particularly as expressed in acts of civil disobedience, has held a controversial place in the life of the church over many centuries. When a church stands up for its convictions in the shadow of the state, it sets a course that often brings swift consequences from the public authorities. Such was the case again and again for the followers of Jesus who established the early church. Jesus reminded his own disciples to "Pay to the Emperor what belongs to the Emperor, and pay to God what belongs to God" (Matthew 22:21b). In the book of Acts, Peter and John defended their own preaching, which was forbidden by public authorities, in saying, "You yourselves judge what is right in God's sight—to obey you or to obey God. For we cannot stop speaking of what we ourselves have seen and heard" (Acts 4:19–20).

+ + +

In the midst of all the controversy surrounding U.S. policy toward Central American refugees during the 1980s, Helena became involved in a sanctuary church in Arizona. "It was there that I realized the church could take its own calling seriously," Helena commented. "The church could stand up for something it believed in and face the tough consequences of its actions. The church of the middle class could do something tangible for people whom Jesus considered 'the least of these' [Matthew 25:40]. To me, this is what the church ought to be—a prophetic voice among its people and throughout the nation. When I saw the church being the church, I was able to believe once again that there was hope for the church."

Helena was the daughter of a preacher. Her father served only one pastorate during her childhood. Over the years, the church members were particularly critical of her mother. Helena's mother had developed strategies for coping with the pettiness she faced within the congregation. Yet as Helena observed these dynamics, they deeply impacted her attitude toward the Christian faith that the church professed. Even at a young age Helena believed that the church failed to live up to the ideals that it preached. This disturbed her deeply.

When it was time to be confirmed at age thirteen, Helena talked to her parents about her serious questions regarding Christianity. She asked them how they would feel if she chose not to complete the confirmation process. "They were very supportive of my desire to follow my conscience," Helena commented, "but I knew it would be a major disappointment to them if I wasn't confirmed. I also knew the church folk would never stop talking about it. My parents would feel it was a deficiency in their parenting and so would the congregation. I finally decided to be confirmed anyway."

Helena caught a glimpse of a different kind of church during her time in Arizona on a summer mission project. Despite these brief experiences, she found it difficult to hold on to this vision when she returned home and then later moved away to college. Helena spent her college years dechurched, dabbling in paganism and various forms of woman-centered spirituality. Encouragement from a close friend was instrumental in leading Helena back to the church. "I still am not convinced that Jesus was also God, but I certainly admire the kind of ministry that Jesus had among the poor and the outcast. I realize what an important part faith convictions play in the lives of people with the courage to tackle the ills of society. I am beginning to make sense of Christianity once again," Helena confessed.

+ + +

When I ask members of the church that my husband and I pastor why they left the church at some point in their lives, the issues of the church's integrity and relevancy repeatedly arise. "I felt the church was too driven by a quest for money to support its own self-perpetuation," said Bertha. "People should be the focus of the church's ministry, not funding," she continued.

A college student named Marty replied, "The church simply didn't speak to the cares and concerns that were important to me. No one wanted to explore issues of wealth and poverty, of economics and justice. I live in one of the wealthiest nations of the world that consumes a vast proportion of the world's resources. To me, this is a faith issue. Even though Jesus talked about money a lot, none of the churches I ever attended grappled with the broad issues of economic stewardship. Our society is given to such materialistic values. These values are often just as evident within the church as in the American culture."

Steve and I are convinced that there are many dechurched Christians on the Oberlin College campus with a similar vision of social justice that propels them to take action in the name of Christ.

They fold into the secular fabric of the university, sporadically interacting with Christian groups or churches throughout the community. Yet their voices need to be heard by the church, and their concerns need to be taken seriously. The community of faith can only benefit from the passionate commitment of such individuals as they seek to live out their journeys of Christian discipleship in a multitude of ways.

+ + +

Twila had a different experience regarding the relevancy of the church than did Helena, Marty, or Bertha. She grew up in a liturgical church where her parents served as active members. During the turbulence of the 1960s a progressive pastor served the church, and Twila's parents left for a more conservative church in a different denomination. Twila is currently active in yet another denomination where her husband serves as a music director.

For the past few years, Twila has been increasingly concerned about the tension within the church between traditional worship styles, characterized by formality, liturgy, and classical music, and modern worship styles noted for their informality, spontaneity, and simple praise choruses. As a woman who finds significant nourishment from traditional worship, Twila sees herself and others like her as being pushed to the margins of the church's life as the congregation seeks to attract newcomers who prefer more contemporary styles of worship. "The church is dechurching many of its older members who have served faithfully for decades," Twila laments, "and no one seems to notice or care."

As the church seeks to become relevant to people within its neighborhood and beyond, Twila raises a serious point. What is the price of this attempt, and how do we embrace the variety of worship styles and traditions that are meaningful to contemporary people? Twila protests, "My complaint is with the theological 'dumbing down' of the church, turning meaningful worship into simply happy-clappy services."

For Twila, the issue of relevancy embraces both theology and worship style. She is not content with a "feel-good Christianity" that hypes her up on Sundays in order to go out into the world with a little extra adrenalin flowing on Monday. Instead, she is searching for substance, depth, and integrity in worship—and all of that within the context of a traditional format.

The needs of people are as varied as we can imagine. For some, emotionalism is a pathway toward connection with God. For others, God is most easily met through deep silence, quiet meditation, or structured worship. Whenever possible, we must take care to avoid dechurching our own in pursuit of those outside the door. With any kind of change, there will inevitably be those who support it and those who do not. Due to the intensity of human difference in theology and practice, change often produces dechurched people. The church would do well in seeking sensitivity to the needs of all its members and searching for ways to address a variety of needs and worship styles.

+ + +

The spiritual relevancy of the church is utterly fundamental to its mission. As my husband and I have sought to work with other churches in developing a vital youth ministry among several small parishes, the issue of spiritual relevancy has repeatedly arisen. "What is the point of offering opportunities for recreation and community service if youth are not exploring the deeper spiritual issues of life?" we ask ourselves. There are numerous secular opportunities for entertainment and adequate avenues for community service, but the religious institutions within any community offer a unique gift— the gift of faith.

Kristene attended church with her family as a child. Her memories of youth group from her teen years primarily revolved around attending events in order to be in the company of a boy whom she liked. At confirmation, she giggled through the ceremony. Years later, she realized that she knew practically nothing about the faith into which she was confirmed. "I didn't know the Bible, why Jesus died for me, or that salvation came through him, or even that I needed to be saved. I had no business being confirmed. I wonder now why nobody noticed or confronted me on that," she confessed. Kristene asked her youth group leaders many questions about Christianity, but she never got any specific answers. Usually she was told, "That's the way it is. It just is." This was never enough to satisfy her probing mind.

Kristene's parents eventually stopped going to church and became exclusively immersed in their favorite social causes. Kristene moved away from Christianity, even though she experienced a gnawing emptiness inside. She briefly visited one church, but quickly discovered that she was expected to be there on Sunday morning, Sunday evening, Wednesday evening, and at Monday night Bible study. The first time she was mildly reproached for missing a service, she stopped going altogether. Throughout her college years, Kristene openly described herself as an "agnostic searching for the truth." She resisted any type of organized religion and despised ritual that could be repeated by rote without any thought or belief whatsoever. Kristene eventually began scoffing at Christians and the church. She felt that they embraced meaningless ideas with no foundation in fact.

A turning point came after Kristene married and her husband joined the military. While he was in basic training, she had to drive nine to eleven hours in order to visit him. Reflecting on these long trips, she mused, "On the way down, there were sets of crosses along the road. There was a large white cross in the middle with two smaller yellow crosses on the sides. The first time down I remember scoffing at the sight of the crosses. By the last trip, I realized that my feelings toward the crosses had changed. I realized that I now had a sense of safety and protection as I passed them. I believe that God was using this time to plant a seed."

A few months after her husband returned from basic training, Kristene met Amy, a young woman having car trouble, whom she and her husband stopped at the roadside to help. Kristene and Amy became friends. Amy didn't mention church, God, Jesus, or Christianity for months. In fact, it was Kristene who eventually brought up her confusion about religion, the validity of the Bible, debates on science-versus-Christianity, and other related topics.

Throughout the ensuing months, Kristene regularly shared her questions with Amy. Amy pondered them carefully and shared scriptures with Kristene that helped her explore the Bible anew. Kristene reflected on this process, "God would lead my heart to some area in which I was in disagreement with God. I would ask Amy. She would answer scripturally. I would still disagree, but go home and ponder it (sometimes unconsciously) until it made sense.

⏱ DAY-TIMER®

BONUS CERTIFICATE

This Certificate good for 15% OFF the online purchase of any item on daytimer.com.
When making a purchase, enter the Certificate # where indicated on the shopping cart order form.
Good toward online purchases only; not transferable, not negotiable.
Day-Timers assumes no responsibility if lost or stolen. Offer expires March 31, 2005.

Promotional Certificate # _____**178689**_____

Printed in USA

E4007

Then I would go to Amy and we would discuss it in more depth. Finally, there was validation for the Christian faith, and there were reasons behind why Christianity was the way it was. It made sense." Kristene eventually began to attend a church where she was able to continue to grow in her faith.

As Kristene recalled her years of being dechurched, she regretted the fact that no one took the time to teach her the importance of the Bible and the authenticity of its witness about God. She felt that many of her questions could have been addressed long ago through studying the scriptures, but no one had led her to the Bible itself for spiritual direction and guidance.

+ + +

Helena was dechurched as she struggled with the lack of social relevancy she experienced within the church. While not dechurched herself, Twila felt burdened by the dechurching of longtime faithful church members as the church pursued new populations outside its doors. Kristene wished that someone had shared the words of life and truth rooted within the biblical testimony many years earlier in her life. The church's relevancy or irrelevancy—both spiritual and social—is often a primary issue among the dechurched.

The burning questions that people face drive them to both search for meaning and reject the answers they receive when these responses are inadequate or superficial. The church must wrestle with the tough issues and probing criticisms that the dechurched bring to any dialogue about Christian faith and practice. We cannot afford to separate the critical needs of the world from our vision for the church. Neither can we seek to be socially relevant without attending wholeheartedly to our spiritual foundations in Christ. Our vision for ministry within the world today calls us to lives of faithfulness in both the spiritual and social realms. Only when we take such integration seriously can we begin to speak to the dechurched around us.

PART III

How Can
the Dechurched
Believe Again?

CHAPTER 10

Stages of Response to Christianity

When I was a newcomer to Oberlin, I found myself in many situations where people asked me, "Who are you, and what do you do?" At the time, I was a pastor's wife, parenting two preschoolers while helping my husband revitalize a small church that was struggling to survive. Further, this church was a *Baptist* church. Upon the revelation of this last fact, the body language of the listener would sometimes change dramatically, and I would guess (usually correctly!) that some difficult life encounter with Baptists had taken place along the way.

One particular night, I was having a very interesting conversation with Sandra while attending a support group for young mothers. She too had preschoolers. While we chatted happily about our children, Sandra asked me why I had moved to Oberlin. As soon as I explained my connection to one of the Baptist churches in town, this young mother literally took two steps backward. Her countenance changed. Her manner became guarded rather than friendly. Her previously animated tone of voice flattened. Sandra looked extremely uncomfortable. I sensed that she wanted to remove herself from our conversation as quickly as possible. Nothing could hide her striking changes in demeanor.

What did Sandra expect me to do to her? I wondered. *What had happened in her life that could lead to such an intense reaction to the word "Baptist"?* I decided then and there that I wanted to get to know this woman. Not only did I like her as a person, but I was driven to understand why she had reacted so forcefully that evening. I knew there must be a hidden story in her past; I just had no idea what it was.

Over the ensuing months, I did indeed spend time with Sandra. She must have wondered whether I would be just like whatever other Baptists she had known. She was most likely terrified that I would invade the privacy of her unpleasant memories.

Eventually, the day came when Sandra and I talked about our first meeting. I told her what I had experienced when I mentioned my affiliation with a Baptist church. She had no idea that her body language had communicated so forcefully. She apologized as she began telling me her life story.

Sandra had grown up in an independent Baptist church among Baptists who banned makeup, movies, dancing, you name it. Church members rejoiced in their own salvation and looked down on all the so-called Christians around them whom they felt had sold their souls to the world, if not to the devil. Sandra's teen years were marked by isolation and depression. She was forbidden to participate in most of the social activities of her classmates. As she faced the bodily changes of puberty and the onset of acne, she was not allowed to cover up any facial blemishes with makeup. For Sandra, this experience was particularly humiliating. She knew she had to do as she was told, but no one could force her to *believe* what she was told.

After leaving home at age eighteen, Sandra began exploring the many activities that had been banned from her childhood. She rejected the strict viewpoints of her Baptist family and church. As the years passed, Sandra increasingly identified herself with a humanist, universalist way of thinking rather than the fundamentalist Baptist perspective of her youth. And then, one day, she found herself at a gathering of young mothers, talking to a Baptist pastor's wife. It had been too much for her.

Years later, I attended a conference where a writer was soliciting the testimonies of men and women raised in fundamentalist homes who had left fundamentalism as adults. The author had developed an extensive questionnaire that offered such individuals the opportunity to explore their spiritual autobiographies. I picked up some extra copies at the conference and gave one to Sandra when I returned home. The questions plumbed the fault lines of childhood experience, gradual changes in thinking, shifts in theological perspective, as well as current beliefs and practices. After working through it, Sandra thanked me profusely for the opportunity to fill it out and reflect more deeply on where she had come from and where she was going.

I don't see much of Sandra these days, but we do bump into each other occasionally. She has never shown up at The First Baptist Church of Oberlin. That doesn't surprise me at all, but I think Sandra has a better sense of who she is because we met. She has helped me to forge a clearer understanding of the kinds of responses that dechurched people have, as well as the stages they pass through in order to believe again. The last time I saw Sandra she said, "You will never realize how important knowing you has been for me. You have really helped me sort out my faith."

+ + +

In working with the dechurched, I have discovered that there are no time limits when it comes to processing damaging experiences from the past. There are also no guarantees that a dechurched person will reclaim his or her Christian faith if that individual has been deeply traumatized in the church or Christian family.

Months ago, I attended an interfaith dialogue. The guest presenter was a Unitarian Universalist (UU) pastor who was raised Baptist. As she described the membership of UU congregations, I was deeply affected by her comments. "The organizing center of our community is not Jesus, as in Christian churches. Rather, it is a sense of mutual acceptance and respect for all types of persons at all sorts of places on their spiritual journeys. Along with this acceptance and respect is a commitment to social justice."

As the pastor continued, she commented on the struggles within UU communities as they attempted to integrate humanists, pagans, feminists, professing Christians, those I describe as the dechurched, and all sorts of other folks attracted to Unitarian Universalist principles. The pastor particularly mentioned how difficult it was for the small percentage of active Christians in the UU and those who have been traumatized in the church to welcome one another and respect the language of one another's faith. I was not surprised. When the church does little to listen to the stories of the dechurched, many of them leave the Christian faith behind in search of totally different expressions of spirituality. The church must acknowledge this reality.

While some leave Christianity for different faiths or no faith at all, others make dramatic shifts from one denomination or style of Christian worship to another. After years of liturgical worship, a person may realize that she or he no longer finds liturgy meaningful as a vehicle for expressing personal faith. On the other hand, someone who has enjoyed years of free, spontaneous worship may discover that liturgy and structure provide needed stability and continuity for serving God. Some may struggle with particular positions of their denomination with which they do not agree. This leaves them feeling marginalized and often causes them to question whether they need to leave their church home and affiliate with a more like-minded body of believers.

For some individuals, raised to believe that their particular brand of Christianity has all the answers and no other church will do, changing allegiances becomes tantamount to spiritual suicide. This creates a difficult struggle that may lead to maintaining an outward church commitment that is inconsistent with the inner beliefs and attitudes they hold. Conversely, the dechurched may make hasty exits from churches that they have faithfully served and leave behind friendships built over many years. At times, they may also distance themselves from their biological families in order to avoid the rejection felt by being labeled heretical or even damned.

Cultural factors that provide ethnic solidarity may reinforce a commitment to a certain denomination or faith perspective. A loss of group identity around cultural distinctions results from leaving deep spiritual roots. The support gained from this experience of community may not be easily replicated.

During several years when dominant theological positions were radically realigned in the Southern Baptist Convention, I attended a conference where a large number of Southern Baptist moderates were present. One such young person named Jeff plaintively confessed to me, "I have been a Southern Baptist all my life. This is my identity. This is who I am. Now my denomination no longer wants people like me. I can't be anything but a Southern Baptist. It is my spiritual and cultural home. What am I to do?"

Jeff's situation was different from that of many dechurched people. Jeff did not want to walk away from the church. Instead, the denomination was moving away from the convictions of Jeff and others like him. In many situations the dechurched face a combination of being marginalized and rejected; they then leave. Sometimes the messages are self-evident, as in Jeff's circumstance. Other times, they are such deafening cultural messages that anyone listening might automatically assume that the church is not a friendly or safe place for them.

+ + +

Anne was an extremely reserved college student. She came to church faithfully Sunday after Sunday and always sat in the second row. She arrived just as the service began and usually left immediately after church, so no one really got a chance to talk with her on Sunday mornings. One summer, Anne left Oberlin as college students usually do, but she never came back to the church in the fall. I wondered what had happened to her. Months later I saw Anne riding her bike down the street. She had lost about forty pounds, cut her hair short, and changed her wardrobe. I waved to her, and she casually acknowledged my greeting as she rode past me.

Ed was among the most active Christian students on campus. He was always eager to reach out to others, and even came up with the idea of starting a Christian book table in the Student Union. He sold his idea to others in his campus fellowship group. Before long, every Friday afternoon, Ed was in the Student Union, staffing the book table and chatting with passing students about issues of Christian faith.

The following year, Ed spent a semester abroad. When he came back to Oberlin, he didn't return to his Christian fellowship group as everyone had expected. Ed didn't even contact a lot of his former Christian friends.

Rhonda really enjoyed her relationships within the church community. She was one of those rare students who was eager to widen her support network beyond the plethora of eighteen- to twenty-two-year-old colleagues with whom she studied and socialized day by day. She frequently attended church potlucks and even joined intergenerational Bible study groups. She was a vibrant young woman from a solid Christian background who had a lot to offer to others.

During Rhonda's junior year of college, she stopped going to church. The transition seemed abrupt to me. I called her, but she just mumbled something about going through "some spiritual struggles" and needing some time away from the church to sort things out. Rhonda had been such an integral part of the church community for so long, it seemed a shame that she didn't feel comfortable sharing her spiritual crisis with anyone at church, even with me.

Rhonda, Ed, and Anne all had one thing in common. These young people each faced a crisis of belonging in the Christian community as they struggled, and ultimately came to grips, with the issue of sexual orientation in their lives. None of them ever talked with me or Steve about this journey. They walked alone, isolated from the support and encouragement of Christian friends, mentors, and peers. Each of them responded to the deafening cultural messages of the institutional church as it screamed, "We don't want to deal with the issue of homosexuality. You no longer belong, get out! Go somewhere else to do your sorting. You are not welcome here!"

In each instance, it ultimately didn't matter whether there were Christians around these young people who could have been trusted. Rhonda, Ed, and Anne could not be convinced that they would be loved unconditionally rather than rejected completely. Each decided it was safer to withdraw from the church than to test its love. None of them ever found out whether their Christian communities would stand beside them or not.

The experiences of Ed, Rhonda, and Anne changed me. They forced me to realize that the church that refuses to engage the issue of homosexuality is no better than the church that openly condemns homosexuals and drives them out of their midst. The active rejection or passive distancing of sincere believers like these three students is happening in churches all over the United States. It is a sobering reality to watch the church litter the landscape with its own wounded. If we were to listen to the stories of people like Ed, Rhonda, and Anne, we might hear their pain and find ourselves transformed in that hearing.

I spoke one day with a pastor who has a gay son. Once again, I was reflecting on the struggles and agonies of those who had left the church and/or lost their faith. This pastor said to me, "When I go to visit my son in San Francisco, it breaks my heart. Literally all of his friends come from Christian families and churches that have disowned them. These young people are so bitter. Christian faith has not been a gift to them. How shall they ever see the love of God, if not in the face of the Christians who bore them and the churches that nurtured them throughout their childhoods?"

As the dechurched encounter particular Christians or Christianity in general, the first stage of their response is usually one of complete alienation. "Leave me alone!" becomes their battle cry. They have had enough of Christians and their pat answers. They have had enough of rigidity and hypocrisy. They have had enough of unexplained suffering. They have had enough of silence, rejection, and abuse. Whatever their experiences, the last thing they want to do is to hang around with Christians.

Sometimes, even when directly addressed, angry dechurched folks will not speak to a person they know is a Christian. Other times, they will make brief, polite conversation, all the while communicating through their body language their obvious hostility and disinterest. They will make sure that no invasion of their privacy occurs.

+ + +

Pastor Jim stopped to see a family who had recently visited his church. A cranky old man sporadically mumbling to himself sat in a living room chair. After saying hello to him, Pastor Jim focused his attention on the young parent who had brought her three children to church the past Sunday. He asked about her and her family. As she began recounting her life story, he listened intently. When Pastor Jim prepared to leave, the old man looked at him and said in a gruff voice, "Well, you paid lots of attention to my granddaughter, but what about me? I'm here, too." Pastor Jim was taken aback, and he quickly apologized. He had no idea that this man wanted to participate in the conversation.

Upon leaving, Jim spent a long time thinking about why he had been so insensitive to the older man. It seemed uncharacteristic for him to respond as he had. Jim began remembering all the dechurched family members of parishioners. Most of them did not speak with him at all when he made pastoral calls to their homes. Jim realized that he had become so accustomed to times when his friendliness was rebuffed by the dechurched that it had never occurred to him to interact with this crotchety old man after offering his initial greetings.

+ + +

People know how to pass along the message "Leave me alone." They may do this by taking several steps backward and becoming distant. They may offer a polite but strained greeting and then proceed to ignore the presence of a guest. They may turn down offers to visit a church, attend its programs, or socialize with certain people. They may even become angry and abusive, verbally insisting that they be left alone.

Many dechurched people will spend years in this first stage of response to their alienation and pain. They never consider the possibility that healing might come if their underlying issues are squarely and seriously engaged. Their whole lives may be characterized by denial and distancing. The masks they wear may grow more elaborate as the years pass. Eventually, they hardly realize what they are reacting to or why they behave as they do. Often they don't even care.

Occasionally, however, someone will break through this shield and stay present in the life of the dechurched regardless of his or her behavior. Such a person's manner must be very gentle and nonthreatening. A Christian must practice the ministry of presence and depend on sparing verbal testimony while building trust. After repeated safe encounters with a Christian, the dechurched may develop some appreciation for that friend or neighbor.

Hopefully, a genuine Christian friend can become a vehicle for breaking down prejudices and stereotypes of Christians in general. These negative attitudes have most likely developed through specific instances of injury, perhaps over years of experience. The hostility, fear, and disdain felt for Christianity may gradually cease to be projected onto this particular friend. At that point, the dechurched may move into the second stage of response, which is one of detached observation. The unspoken confession is this: "I will observe you, but I am going to keep my distance."

+ + +

Betty shared with me the gradual transformation of her attitude toward Christians. "I left the church ten years ago at the age of fourteen. My family was very faithful in attending services, but we moved and never joined another church. I even looked around for a church with my friends. I visited several of the places they worshiped. One church really frightened me with all its emotionalism and its strategy of scaring kids into accepting Christ. Nothing seemed to really fit me, so I gave up the search. After a while, I just stopped thinking about religion at all."

She continued, "In college I majored in philosophy. I was really down on Christians and Christianity in general. That changed when I became friends with a voice major who was a devout Christian. Her life seemed so different from mine. She had a cohesive center out of which she made her decisions and looked at the world. Everything in her life fit around that center. I grew to admire her consistency and commitment to Christ. She made me rethink the way I had been looking at Christians. I sort of envied the faith that she had. Why did she have that faith and I did not?"

Betty's experience with her friend began to open her up once again to the possibility of faith. By simply being present and allowing Betty to observe the way she lived, this Christian student had a profound influence on Betty's life.

+ + +

Eric met me for lunch one day. I had always been intrigued by the hints of spiritual longing I detected in his life. He seemed, on the one hand, drawn to religious interests, while on the other hand, he seemed strangely averse to religion. I shared these simple observations with Eric, and he seemed to genuinely welcome the opportunity to talk.

Eric's grandfather had been a pastor. Eric's father rejected his own father's strictness, as well as his father's faith. Eric's parents raised their children with no exposure to Christianity whatsoever. Yet in Eric's heart there was an unsatisfied hunger, perhaps even a memory of faith from prior generations.

Eric described his forays into the realm of spirituality, both as a religion major in college and as a person who explored various faiths, almost as if they were hobbies. Finally, Eric described himself to me as a "religious tourist," nibbling, dabbling, experimenting, and tasting, but never really committing himself to any particular expression of faith, Christian or otherwise.

I have discovered, time and time again, that the second-generation dechurched are often completely unchurched. Their parents avoid church, Christianity, Christians, and anything else that reminds them of their own unresolved faith issues. As these parents spend their child-rearing years in the first stage of the dechurched, characterized by alienation from Christianity, they pass on to their children a haunting and unfinished legacy.

The tourist mentality that Eric identified is very similar to the second stage of response evidenced among the dechurched. The dechurched open up enough to observe the life of faith, but not enough to become engaged in it themselves. This season of observation provides a sense of both exploration and safety. There are no commitments, thus no pain. There are no decisions, thus no consequences. There are no enduring relationships, thus no heartbreak or betrayal. All the challenges of working through the issues that have led to being dechurched, whether in one's own generation or generations removed, remain untouched in this stage of response.

For the person who interacts with the dechurched, this stage is easier to deal with than the first. At least it is possible to participate in a decent conversation and say more than hello to the individual in question. A Christian acquaintance can even express her or his faith in actions and have such behaviors tolerated or at times even appreciated. The dechurched may ask Christians for prayer support even though they would never pray for themselves and aren't convinced that prayer actually makes a difference. Yet in this stage the dechurched still frequently remain uncomfortable around Christians talking about their faith.

+ + +

Karina, Debbie, and Marge became friends when their children were preschoolers. It wasn't long before Marge told Karina and Debbie that her husband, Rick, was antagonistic toward Christianity. Rick wasn't a believer, yet he had faced more than his share of Christians looking for new converts. He had spent several years serving faithfully in the church while harboring a secret skepticism that eventually surfaced and hardened into an antipathy toward "born-again" Christians. Marge had spent much of her life trying to find Christian fellowship for herself while also attempting to keep a clear separation between her life of faith and Rick's determination to avoid any personal talk about Christianity.

Karina and Debbie began praying for Marge and Rick. They knew how difficult it was for Marge to nurture her own faith privately while maintaining the secular family life that Rick demanded. Debbie and Karina's families frequently ate dinner together, but Marge's husband didn't even like being around Christians. How could God break through Rick's general aversion to Christianity and his particular disinterest in getting to know Marge's Christian friends? The three women had no idea.

Meanwhile, each of the women frequently felt overwhelmed by household tasks and childcare needs. All three were stay-at-home moms whose days grew longer and patience grew thinner as evening approached. It was challenging to keep up with the housecleaning while toddlers were constantly making messes.

One day, Marge, Karina, and Debbie came up with a plan to make their lives with their preschoolers easier and more fun. They would meet at each home once a week for a few hours a day. Two of them would clean the house while the other woman would watch all the children. This way, they could be together while also accomplishing necessary tasks. They implemented their plan. Three times each week they happily conversed and enjoyed one another's company while they worked and supervised their children's play. The friendships of their little ones blossomed even as their fellowship with one another deepened.

One day Rick got off work early and arrived home while the women were still working together. He was amazed when he learned what they had been doing. *Why would they do this?* Rick wondered. *There couldn't be any normal explanation for such behavior,* he mused. *It seems like Marge, Debbie, and Karina really care about each other. Otherwise, what could possibly motivate them to voluntarily clean each other's houses and watch each other's kids?* Rick asked himself.

It didn't take words to open Rick to the message of the gospel he had rejected for many years. In fact, words would only have reinforced Rick's constant demands to be left alone. As Rick saw Karina, Debbie, and Marge acting out the love of Christ in this most simple and disarming way, he slowly began warming up to these relationships that had become important to his wife. Within a year, three families—not two—were getting together for dinner.

+ + +

The period of observation for the dechurched is extremely important because it often provides the bridge between the anger and denial of stage one and the emerging openness that accompanies stage three. However long it may last, this period allows trust to develop slowly and cautiously. It offers a person the opportunity to move at his or her own pace in surfacing the personal issues that are associated with people of faith, the church, or Christianity in general.

Countless numbers of individuals never make it past these first two stages of response, and this is a great tragedy for the church. Few Christians are sensitized to the complex dynamics that can exist in loving and reaching out to the dechurched. Further, few dechurched individuals accept the challenge of facing their pain and truly reconstructing their faith. The first two stages of response are relatively safe stages for the dechurched. Neither of these demands the level of openness and commitment that the final two stages require. For this reason, it is easy to remain for years—or even a lifetime—alienated from Christianity or merely touring the religious landscape without ever stopping to search for "home."

+ + +

During the past several years my husband and I have hosted cookie bakes for Oberlin College students at our house. These events have been great opportunities to laugh, converse, sample cookie dough, sing in the kitchen, and generally provide a much-needed break from the daily stresses of student life. Attendance at cookie bakes has waned over the years as students have chosen to study, attend concerts, or do just about anything but gather for such recreation. Although cookie bakes once brought fifteen or twenty students to our home, the time came when six was a good crowd.

One evening, Misha brought Won, a friend of hers, to the cookie bake. Steve and I had never before met this young man. No other students came that night. Without a crowd for cooking, the four of us settled in the living room for what seemed at first to be a get-acquainted chat with Misha's friend.

Won began telling his story. We quickly realized that this young man had faced a tortured and painful faith journey. His parents had been caught up in a cultlike fellowship for years. They served in numerous leadership capacities. Won was torn between his intense feelings of confusion around his own beliefs, the guilt that accompanied his rejection of the faith of his parents, and his deep fear about his family's situation now that he was far away from home. We talked for hours.

I explained to Won what little I had come to understand about the realities of the dechurched and the difficult struggle of reconstructing one's faith and believing again. He was very interested in the topic and requested copies of the few articles I had found that I often use in counseling those who have left the church and/ or their faith.

Misha hadn't bargained for an intense night of theological discussion—she just wanted to bake cookies. So she flitted off to hang out with our daughters while Steve and I continued to unearth the pain, doubt, trauma, and anxiety that mingled in the life of Won. I doubt that he anticipated sharing his story that night with two Baptist pastors he had never before met, but his was a story I will never forget. A few days later, I collected my articles and mailed them to Won along with a letter encouraging him to persist in his complicated struggle with faith and disbelief. I never heard from him again.

+ + +

For some reason, God brought Won to that cookie bake, and this young man seized an opportunity to share a story that had roamed around in his heart like a simmering fire. Perhaps he could not find another safe space to share it, and a stranger's home became an unexpected gift. His solitary act exemplifies the initial efforts at communication that begin to occur in the third stage of response among the dechurched. The underlying message offered is this: "I want to share my pain."

The dechurched person begins to shift from detached observer to confessor. Numerous obstacles to healing quickly surface. The pain can be too deep. The questions can be too numerous. The doubt and confusion can be too overwhelming. The journey can seem too confusing. When the dechurched have been taught to either totally accept the faith system offered to them or face the possibility of automatic damnation, the guilt and conflict over making such a choice can be too much to bear. All these feelings and many more rapidly arise when stories are shared. It is often easier to return to the first two stages than to fully enter the third stage of response. It is much more comfortable to stay forever the observer or the angry person in denial, than it is to share one's pain.

The dechurched individual in this third stage may need extensive counseling, both spiritual and psychological. I often do spiritual counseling with the dechurched while they also meet with a professional counselor who helps them untangle personal and family issues. Many professional counselors are unskilled in dealing with the spiritual journeys of this population. They may minimize faith issues or treat their clients' spiritual autobiographies as pathologies rather than cries of the heart for healing and renewed faith.

Veronica, a clinical psychologist, approached me one day and said, "Do you do a lot of pastoral counseling? I am competent in dealing with most aspects of my clients' lives except faith issues. I am just not a person of faith, and I don't always know where to take those issues in counseling. Actually, I don't think anyone on my staff does. We see a lot of Christians, though, as well as others to whom faith is or once was important."

I appreciated Veronica's honesty with me, but I was grieved by the lack of expertise among her staff regarding issues of spirituality.

Spiritual and psychological histories are intricately woven within a person's life. To tackle one without an understanding of the other is, at best, an incomplete and crippled process.

This does not mean, however, that Christians always benefit the most by seeing only Christian counselors. Christian counselors can at times be equally guilty of addressing everything in a purely spiritual manner, thus minimizing the complexity of psychological issues a person faces. Unfortunately, I have seen this occur as well.

Each individual must seek out his or her own appropriate blend of support on the journey toward renewed faith. This may mean seeing a pastor or pastoral counselor for spiritual direction and another type of helping professional for psychological support. At times this assistance may be available through one special person or a combination of individual and small-group experiences. Each journey is unique and requires its own thoughtful blend of resources.

+ + +

Pam came to my office one day to share her story of confusion and pain caused throughout her young life by the behavior of her mentally ill parent. She wanted to work through some spiritual questions. At the same time, she was seeing a psychologist on a weekly basis in order to unravel complicated family dynamics. Pam and I spent several weeks together exploring the impact of mental illness within her family and how its presence affected Pam's understanding of God and her confusion about the Bible.

Gary, on the other hand, discovered that the best place for him to work on his addiction to alcohol and drugs was in a twelve-step group, Alcoholics Anonymous (AA). He didn't have the insurance coverage for an intensive inpatient treatment program, and he had heard about the effectiveness of this program. In AA, he safely struggled to establish and maintain his sobriety. Gary began to face the difficulties of his past as well as the poor choices he had made. For Gary, the AA group became the first place he ever told his own story of faith, doubt, rebellion, and remorse. As Gary explored the past, he sensed a renewed trust in God growing quietly within his soul. After decades of absence, Gary returned to the church. He found additional support there from the pastor and members of the congregation.

A crisis forced Sally to deal with her mental illness. Sally's paranoia had spiraled out of control. One day, she became so verbally abusive that her neighbors called the police. Sally was taken to a psychiatric facility for emergency stabilization. Her symptoms were treated with medication and counseling. After staying there for a few weeks, Sally was released to her home. Mental health professionals continued to regularly monitor her use of medication as well as her general progress. Contacts between the clergy and the hospital staff proved helpful in offering insight regarding the best ways to support Sally as she sought to become more functional.

Today Sally can talk about her mental illness and how it has affected her life and faith. There was a time, however, when it constantly influenced what she said and did, yet she could not acknowledge its existence. Sally's newfound ability to accept the fact that she struggles with mental illness helps both herself and her children as all of them seek to follow Christ.

+ + +

Every individual has unique needs that must be addressed in a variety of ways. The more support systems a person has, the better the chances are that he or she will survive the point of crisis and move on toward greater health and integration between the disparate parts of life.

The final stage of response among the dechurched is characterized by determination and commitment as the individual shifts from simply communicating her or his pain to fully engaging in the process of healing. The dechurched person's confession at this stage is: "I want to reconstruct my faith." This is an incredibly courageous response. The vast majority of dechurched people never move through the stages of alienation, observation, and communication to this point of engagement. Most languish at some earlier stage that requires less of them. I could never minimize the intensity of this final stage, nor could I minimize the challenge inherent in beginning this task. A faith that is reconstructed and owned is a faith that is reclaimed from the clutches of injury, betrayal, addiction, or a host of other factors. It is a faith worth having, keeping, and sharing with others.

A few years ago, I led a series of Bible studies at a national evangelism meeting for denominational staff persons and pastors. There were only a handful of women in the mostly male audience, middle-aged and older. As I walked out of the room after completing my first Bible study, a professor of pastoral counseling at a Baptist seminary stopped me. He commented, "I am amazed that you are still a Christian."

My surprise at this response registered immediately on my face. The professor noted my reaction and went on to say, "You have done so much work to find your own story within the scriptures and reconstruct your understanding of the faith again and again. You have overcome many obstacles along the way. Most people with your story would have already given up on Christianity."

Many circumstances that I have ultimately navigated as a person of faith have left countless others dechurched. Yet to me, leaving my faith was never an option. My response to this man's words came straight from my heart as I replied, "I could never give up on Christianity, because Jesus means too much to me. He has been my friend and companion through all my searching and growing. I wrestle with the scriptures and don't let them go until they speak to me anew time and time again."

CHAPTER 11

Engaging in Personal Healing and Recovery

The journey toward a rebuilt faith cannot merely address the obvious. It must plumb the depths that lie beneath the surface of life. Oftentimes, layers of personal hurt and betrayal are discovered there. Each layer in turn must be addressed in order for healing to occur. The process of dismantling and reconstructing one's relationship with God is an intense, difficult, and wonderful journey. It is the hope and goal of ministry among the dechurched.

Engaging in a process of personal healing and recovery is a fundamental step toward rebuilding an enduring faith. Any history of trauma, abuse, addiction, or mental illness must be uncovered and explored. It is easy for a broken individual to focus his or her anger on a denomination, a group of people, a particular church, Christianity, or Christians in general. For new life to grow, that person must acknowledge his or her own vulnerability, anger, shame, and confusion.

It is equally important to face one's own denial or even rage. A host of emotions can lodge deep within the hearts of the dechurched, and these feelings need to be named and explored. Issues that at first glance may seem vague and diffuse are often in fact very specific.

+ + +

Lenny became a casualty of a very painful church split. He, like many others, left the church he loved over a controversy regarding the expression of various spiritual gifts during worship. Initially, he was furious with God for allowing this to happen. Over time, his anger distilled into bitterness. Eventually, Lenny completely closed himself off from his spiritual thoughts and feelings. Years later, Lenny's attitudes about Christianity were acidic.

While socializing with his buddies in the workplace, Lenny often made unkind jokes about Christians. His comments really bothered Evan, who was a devout Christian. Evan had no idea why Lenny was so negative toward Christianity. Concerned that Lenny might blow up, Evan was hesitant to broach the subject. He had no idea that Lenny's hostility masked a prior commitment to Christ and the church as well as a deep unresolved pain surrounding this commitment.

Lenny had never processed his feelings about the church split, nor had he examined how this experience had impacted his relationship with God. Over the years, he generalized these very specific hurts and projected them onto all Christians and all churches. If Lenny were to reexamine his own spiritual history, perhaps he could untangle some critical issues of faith.

Lenny needs to identify specific issues of unresolved spiritual conflict that cry out for reflection and healing. He needs to reconsider the interpersonal and theological aspects of the church split and how he responded to it when it actually occurred. Does one church split imply that all churches are bad? Does Lenny's experience with this one church in the past mean that no Christian can ever be trusted? To explore such questions would be an enormous step in Lenny's life. This rethinking process could help Lenny recognize that his vague but intense hostility toward all Christians is in fact a direct response to his own particular woundedness.

+ + +

Mariana shared difficult confidences about her personal life with a dear Christian friend, Tracey. A few weeks later a friend of Tracey's whom Mariana had never met confronted Mariana in public and demanded to know whether these confidences were true. Mariana was stunned. She had never told her story to this stranger. How did this woman even know about the struggles that Mariana faced?

It didn't take long for Mariana to realize that Tracey had been sharing Mariana's story with others. Mariana felt horribly betrayed. She asked Tracey to meet with her because she wanted to get to the bottom of the situation. Tracey put her off time and time again. Mariana felt forced to distance herself from this friend and confidante whom she had once trusted completely.

The damaged relationship took its toll on Mariana. She became fearful, suspicious, and bitter. She began struggling with feelings of depression that she had never previously experienced. She began doubting her ability to discern whom she could truly trust and whom she should not. Mariana also felt violated by God. Within a few months of the incident, Mariana's entire relationship with Christ and other Christians was significantly altered.

Mariana had grown up in the church and had never experienced the harsh pain that accompanies betrayal. Her upbringing in the church had had its rough moments, but overall Mariana had known many good Christian people whom she had counted on without question. Her relationship with God had been solid, even amid the many changes and transitions that often occur in young adulthood. The entire foundation of Mariana's faith that had been built over the past twenty years seemed perilously close to collapse.

Before the pain of betrayal hardens into complete alienation from the God Mariana so faithfully followed her entire life, this young woman would do well to explore some critical questions. Who broke her trust, and who did not? How did Mariana deal with this devastating incident initially, as well as weeks later when she had to acknowledge that Tracey refused to talk about the situation? How did the lack of resolution of this conflict impact Mariana's relationships with other Christians and with Christ? What possibilities for healing exist if Mariana cannot experience reconciliation—or even communication—with Tracey herself? How has the whole situation affected Mariana's understanding of herself as a beloved child of God?

+ + +

These types of explorations are critical in helping the dechurched—or the nearly dechurched—begin the process of personal healing and recovery. Behind each leave-taking is a story of tremendous significance. That story, as painful or sordid as it might be, begs to be unearthed, reopened, shared, and faced in the light of God's love and grace.

Written resources also exist that can help the dechurched rediscover their faith. Recovery literature can be particularly valuable for those who have been impacted by dysfunctional families or church structures. Twelve-step programs such as Alcoholics Anonymous, Codependents Anonymous, and Alanon can provide safe places for honesty, confession, and accountability while an individual tackles patterns of self-defeating behavior.

Years ago, I led two groups of women through Melody Beattie's book *Codependent No More.* At least a third of the women who came had left the church after at one time being active participants. Many of these women had begun the journey from disbelief back to faith through twelve-step programs. In these contexts, God was referred to as a "higher power." For them, this was a safe way to speak about a strengthening agent beyond the self.

These women could not use the traditional language of the church to name God at this point in their lives. Yet many still longed to personally acknowledge a transcendent reality and confess their need for a power beyond themselves. Some Christians reject twelve-step programs and chafe at referring to God as a "higher power" for fear of claiming anything as a higher power. The fact remains that twelve-step programs continue to be instrumental in reaching the dechurched in ways that many churches have not.

The women in the recovery groups I led who had participated in twelve-step programs were much more able to talk about their failures, struggles, and family secrets than were the attending churchgoers who had grown accustomed to protecting their self-images within their congregations. Those who had rediscovered their faith in the safe and confidential environment of twelve-step programs were witnesses to the effective outreach of these groups among the dechurched, in spite of the fact that such programs specifically avoid formulating outreach strategies.

Many other recovery resources exist, from articles to books, from workshops to conferences. Those that help Christians look at the dynamics of dysfunctional families, issues of spiritual abuse and addiction, as well as ways to explore scripture anew, are invaluable aids for the dechurched seeking to regain their faith.

CHAPTER 12

Identifying Systemic Issues in Recovery

In spite of the fact that one's personal healing and recovery can sometimes take months or even years, the dechurched discover that there is more to examine than the individual journey alone. Oftentimes, the path toward a reconstructed faith includes identifying systemic social issues evidenced within one's situation. I observed this reality most clearly one day as I made three different pastoral calls to women of various ages.

My morning began with a breakfast meeting. I met Darla at a local restaurant. She was a single mother whose ex-husband, Bill, chose to maintain little contact with his young children. The two sons were keenly aware of their father's disinterest in their lives. They acted out their feelings of rejection in a host of ways that made parenting enormously challenging for Darla.

Darla was barely making ends meet. She and Bill spent many afternoons in domestic court arguing over childcare payments. Bill was both self-employed and underemployed, so his financial contributions were minimal. Collections were sporadic at best. Meanwhile, Darla was locked into a job that used only a small portion of her many talents. She rationalized her lack of vocational opportunities by reminding herself, "At least I have a steady income and health insurance for myself and the kids."

After breakfast, I stopped by to see Alice, an older woman recovering from an emergency appendectomy. The only help she could get from family members during her recuperation came from other women in her family. Alice's husband "didn't do house-cleaning." Actually, none of the males in the family did. They didn't cook either. Alice's niece traveled several miles each day to assist her aunt with the housework that Alice could not attend to herself.

Finally, I visited Edna, a retired woman in her seventies. In an effort to be faithful to her marital vows, she had long endured a difficult marriage to Arty, an alcoholic. One day Edna decided that she had simply had enough. She packed up her bags and left to visit her sister in another state. After nearly fifty years of marriage, she refused to return home until she renegotiated aspects of her relationship with Arty.

Edna hadn't gone to church for years because Arty refused to go with her. She felt that going alone would just add more stress to her relationship with Arty than she already faced. Edna compromised on this by getting up early on Sunday mornings to watch religious programming on television while Arty slept late. Edna made do, just as her own mother and grandmother had taught her.

When I ended my day, I was struck by how different each of these stories was, yet how similar the themes were that bound them together. Strict gender roles in combination with a lack of male responsibility deeply impacted each of these women and their families. In every instance, the female found herself trapped in a situation of chronic overfunctioning. Darla, Alice, and Edna consistently compensated for the lack of commitment expressed by the males within their family systems.

I reflected for a while on the abuses that occur when family roles are locked into tight patterns of female submission and male dominance. Divorce and spousal nonsupport, absentee fathers, and inflexible male/female roles that assign all caregiving duties to women are among numerous issues that are systemic in nature and widely evident in contemporary Western culture. Many persons in recovery address their own particular circumstances without ever acknowledging the larger social issues that frame their experiences. Placing one's own situation within a broader context can help a person feel less isolated. Many who suffer in silence believe that no one else could possibly understand what they are experiencing. Oftentimes, kindred spirits are right around the corner.

I will never forget the day, years ago, when a college student named Irene stood up during our prayer and sharing time at a Sunday church service. Irene confessed that she was feeling suicidal and needed a lot of support. My husband, Steve, was leading the service. He reacted quickly, asking all those who felt moved to head upstairs to a small prayer room and surround Irene with prayer. As I watched individuals rise from their pews to leave with this young woman, I was profoundly touched. Each of these persons—male and female, young and old—had also struggled with depression and thoughts of suicide. Yet none of them had ever shared their private pain with anyone else in the church except Steve or me. Here was a lone college student, brave enough to speak the truth of her struggle. Through her shared vulnerability, Irene led the way for others to realize that they, too, were not alone.

+ + +

Support groups focusing around particular needs can provide helpful structures for exploring personal healing and systemic social issues inherent within a person's story. Sometimes the empowerment received from such groups nurtures a vision for social transformation. When the dechurched are able to identify the structural issues that interface their personal woundedness, they may be able to channel their anger and pain into social change that can benefit large groups of survivors who experience similar difficulties.

Public advocacy can become an important aspect of healing for the person seeking to make sense of his or her circumstances. It can also be beneficial to the world beyond one's own doors. An unwed father named Jake turns his life around. He studies his social context and realizes that he is only one among a sea of others who have taken little or no responsibility for nurturing their offspring. He begins volunteering for an organization that takes a long, hard look at the importance of fathers in the lives of children. The nonprofit agency connects underemployed fathers lacking in job skills with job training programs and interviewing resources. Classes are held to help fathers develop healthy parenting skills. Topics of shared custody, responsible financial support, and good communication with the ex-spouses or former girlfriends are discussed in small support groups. The systemic nature of issues experienced in an intensely personal context is analyzed and articulated. Jake's own healing is empowered by his participation in the transformation of other men's lives.

Other examples of pain transformed into public advocacy abound, both inside and outside the church. I am reminded of the national crusade to locate missing children, begun by a father whose own son was murdered after disappearing in a shopping center. Parents of a daughter who lay comatose and brain-dead for months on end were instrumental in helping legislators understand the need for guidelines to direct end-of-life medical decisions and to develop appropriate regulations for the use of technology in the continuation of life. Families of plane-crash victims often become powerful voices for heightened standards of airline safety. We can never erase our pain, but it most certainly can be redeemed. The tragedies we face can become agents of reconciliation, healing, and social change on behalf of others. Personal and systemic issues demand equal attention within the healing processes of the dechurched.

+ + +

Myesha is an African American woman in her early twenties who sincerely questions her Christian upbringing. She attended Christian schools throughout her childhood. There she regularly gazed upon pictures of a Jesus marked by obvious European features. Myesha grew up imagining Jesus to be just like the man in those pictures.

At college, Myesha immersed herself in explorations of history and literature. She peered deeply into her own ethnicity and its impact on her life choices. As time passed, Myesha found herself reacting strongly to her European image of Jesus. She began exploring other faiths, particularly African indigenous religions and paganism. Myesha was attracted to their distance from the heritage of white Christianity, which she found so objectionable.

If Myesha is ever going to reconstruct her faith as an African American Christian, she needs to face head-on her reactions to an American Christianity heavily influenced by European images and perspectives. She also needs to address incidents of racism within the church that have reinforced her conviction that Christianity is a racist religion. She must search for additional role models in the Bible, exploring biblical characters with a heightened sensitivity to issues of race and ethnicity.

It will not help Myesha at all if the Christians she knows consider the struggles and questions of her faith to be trivial or mere distractions from following Christ. Her questions have everything to do with what kind of Christ Christians have followed, still do follow, and what kind of Christ she could or would follow. Myesha is searching for a faith that resonates with her own history and addresses her legitimate complaints about Christianity's history of collusion with racism. Myesha cannot settle for a faith that is merely transmitted to her from cultural expressions of Christianity that bear no resemblance to her own experience.

Any pastor or friend who desires to support Myesha in the journey of reconstructing her faith must engage her fully and honestly in serious dialogue. Myesha's objections to Christianity are intensely personal yet also deeply systemic.

+ + +

The church often opts for a solely personalized message of salvation and deliverance from personal pain without taking the time for critical social analysis about the nature and roots of that pain. It is not enough to generically label all pain as individual sin. The personal and social are intricately linked and must both be addressed in the healing and recovery of the dechurched.

All will not embrace public advocacy as a vehicle of grace and a pathway toward renewed hope and meaning. Some, however, will. For these, the integration of the personal and the systemic will offer a much-needed catalyst in breaking the power that their deep woundedness holds over their lives. Their pain can be transformed into action for the public good. Support can be found from others who have faced similar circumstances. The wounded are no longer alone. They have a mission and purpose for living.

CHAPTER 13

Detoxifying the Bible

Even while the dechurched explore personal and systemic issues of healing and recovery, these alone are insufficient in guiding the dechurched toward a reconstructed faith. The dechurched must begin an often long and challenging process of reexamining biblical interpretation and, literally, detoxifying the messages they have received from the Bible.

Myesha struggles with the racism she has encountered in the church. She cannot reconcile the concept of a loving God with the behaviors of the prejudiced Christians she has encountered. Further, she cannot reconcile the scriptures she reads in Ephesians about slaves and masters with her deep commitment to human equality. Moreover, she cannot stomach the way these scriptures have been used historically to demean, oppress, and marginalize African Americans throughout the history of the United States.

Myesha will never retain her Christian faith without seriously wrestling with the Bible. She is at a critical turning point in her thinking and exploring. Her life is crying out for a faith that speaks to her own history and experience. To develop this kind of faith, she must lay bare her understanding of scripture up to this point and explore anew this text that she has read numerous times in the past.

The Bible must speak to Myesha in fresh ways. It must address her need to confront the social injustice of racism as she experiences it, faces it, and reflects on it. The prophetic power of the Bible to speak to the concerns of the marginalized and oppressed must be reclaimed. The images of a mild, docile, and *white* Jesus that roam in Myesha's mind must be challenged. Texts such as the one in Colossians 3:22 that states, "Slaves, obey your human masters in all things, not only when they are watching you because you want to gain their approval; but do it with a sincere heart because of your reverence for the Lord" must be confronted, both in their biblical context and in their historical use. The sins of the church must be laid bare and acknowledged.

Contemporary biblical scholars have reexamined issues of ethnicity and race within the scriptures. They have uncovered a richness of diversity that has previously been left unrecognized and unnoticed. Thankfully, resources abound that can help young people such as Myesha forge an understanding of Christian faith that can hold up to intense questioning and challenge escalating cynicism.

Myesha must also reclaim the voices of faith that have stood against racism throughout the history of the church. These voices are numerous, even if at times they seem clouded by those who have supported the status quo and maintained oppressive systems in the name of God. The Bible has been used as an instrument of both liberation and oppression in the history of the church. While difficult to face, acknowledging this reality can be liberating for the dechurched seeking to make sense of the inconsistencies of Christian practice.

It is only when Myesha is invited to deconstruct her understanding of the Bible and expose herself to radically new understandings of its meaning and message that she has the possibility of remaining a Christian. Unless she undertakes this journey, Myesha's faith is in danger of collapsing under the legitimate questions it bears.

+ + +

Leanna was raised in an intensely religious environment. Her biblical training was thorough, filled with detailed studies of church doctrine based on numerous scriptural references. Leanna was taught that her denomination was the only true Christian church, and it alone possessed the "keys to the kingdom of God." Bible verses supported every doctrine that she memorized as a little girl.

Guilt and shame regularly plagued Leanna as this sensitive child tried to live up to the messages she was taught. It seemed that the life of faith should bring joy, yet Leanna felt only recrimination. As she grew, she couldn't wait to leave home and get away from all her confusion. She quietly waited for that day, sure that when she finally left home, she could reject all the guilt and shame the religious faith of her childhood engendered and start over again with God.

The problem was that "home" never left Leanna. It was trapped inside her head and heart and wouldn't let go. At college, Leanna wanted to visit various churches and hear other understandings of God, but she was terrified that her disloyalty would lead to her damnation. She wanted to think about new ideas, but as soon as she did, all the memorized scripture passages of her youth, the pages and pages of outlined theology studied in Bible class, and the rationales for her denomination's exclusive claim to truth flooded her mind. She felt paralyzed.

Leanna made brief forays into questioning, but she found that even this was too overwhelming for her. Her questions were followed by bad dreams at night, which then haunted her days. If she left her childhood faith, her whole family would surely reject her. Even if they didn't, Leanna was certain that all the church folk from home would. Was it better for Leanna to remain confused, shamed, and guilty than to try to sort out what she really believed about God? Leanna was beginning to feel as if she would spend the rest of her life cursed with an inability to either embrace the faith of her childhood or break away from it. She was completely miserable. So many of her college friends didn't even *care* about faith issues, and yet Leanna couldn't escape feeling tortured by them day after day.

Leanna must confront the powerful and often conflicting feelings that accompany the process of reconstructing one's faith. Otherwise, these factors will overtake her desire for growth and leave her stuck where she is. Many people, even devoid of genuine belief, find it easier to retain what is familiar than to search for an authentic faith that is yet unformed.

+ + +

Years ago, I began seminary amid the tug-of-war within my soul between traditional views on the role of women in the church and my sense of calling to full partnership in ministry. Throughout my seminary studies, I did nearly every research project I could on issues of women in the Bible. I explored topics related to gender and Christian theology. I studied the female coworkers of the apostle Paul as mentioned in passages such as Romans 16, Philippians 4, 1 Corinthians 16, and Acts 18. I wrote a Bible study guide for women titled *Jesus, Women, and Me.* I developed study questions that created a three-way dialogue between Jesus, the women around Jesus, and ourselves as women of faith.

My yearning to wrestle with the scriptures and the church's history on issues of women and faith did not stop there. I compared various interpretations of the creation stories in Genesis 1—2 for a theology class and examined their impact on contemporary understandings of gender roles within the church and home. My research paper for a course in world religions explored women in Islam. The last paper I wrote during my seminary years addressed issues of violence in homes where religious beliefs were contributing factors to that violence. I studied the methods of biblical interpretation used to reinforce such abuse perpetrated in the name of God. I looked at ways to recover the Bible in the lives of those damaged by such understandings of scripture. I interviewed a Christian woman in a difficult marriage as she dealt with these issues on a practical rather than theoretical level.

In short, I spent eight years of my life unearthing biblical texts, translations, and history that I had never before noticed or been taught, in spite of the fact that I grew up in the church and had been an active Bible reader for more than a decade. It was through this deep inner struggle of trying to take both the scriptures and my life experience seriously that I gradually reconstructed my faith and embraced my call to ministry.

I made a similar journey years later as I began dealing with issues of self-care in ministry. A struggle with clinical depression drove me into counseling at the age of thirty. I quickly discovered that my concept of Christian servanthood was a primary culprit in my tendency to neglect my own needs for the sake of others. Again, I had to go back to the scriptures and "find myself anew" in its pages. Through studying how Jesus responded in situations of ministry, conflict, friendship, and stress, I sought to discover for myself the kind of balance between selfhood and servanthood that kept Jesus focused, active, and capable of balancing his own needs with those of others. Out of this journey came my first book, *The Road Toward Wholeness: Biblical Meditations for the Recovery Journey,* published by Judson Press.

Serious questions of faith and biblical interpretation confront both the churched and the dechurched. We must ask ourselves, How does a person rebuild a shattered faith and a broken relationship with the Bible, the book of our faith? How does one reenter the world of the church after being away from it for years? Where can an individual encounter the unconditional love of God, if not among the fellowship of Christian believers? The answers to these questions speak to the very core of the nature and mission of the church in the world.

CHAPTER 14

Reworking Theological Understanding

The final area of importance in reconstructing one's faith is reworking inadequate theological understandings. Christians often harbor unspoken assumptions about their faith or about God. For example, some are mistakenly taught that they will be sheltered from tragedy and sorrow if they give their lives to Christ. For a while, this belief may seem to work. However, when a parent dies, a financial crisis hits, or a senseless accident occurs, the believer begins questioning the goodness of God.

I often talk with young people who fall into a trap laid by their own inexperience with life's ups and downs. They reason, "This bad thing happened to me. If God loved me, it wouldn't have occurred. How can anyone believe in a God of love when bad things happen to well-meaning and faithful people?"

I remind these young adults that terrible things happen all over the world all the time to people of faith and to people of no faith. The nature of the global human experience is not altered just because tragedy finally visits our own lives. Further, I try to encourage such individuals to tear down the false assumption that they uniquely

117

deserve divine protection simply because they are Christians. I seek to help them begin to develop a theology and understanding of suffering that can withstand the setbacks and traumas of life. A Christian faith that is not strong enough to survive such difficulties is not a faith worth keeping. Further, it is never a faith that can last.

Suffering is a basic fact of life for people all over the world. Much of the world's population faces daily threats of malnutrition and untreated disease. People in many nations live without freedom and opportunity. Natural disasters such as cyclones, famines, earthquakes, and floods ravage whole towns and kill massive numbers of people. Violence in our nation's cities and towns often strikes the most unsuspecting. While we may know this intellectually, it is different when disaster touches our own lives. Untested theological systems that worked well in times of prosperity and ease are exposed as woefully inadequate in times of tragedy and want.

It is not uncommon for people to become disillusioned and dechurched when their old beliefs no longer work yet new beliefs remain unformed. Individuals at this critical point of transition in their faith need to be encouraged to thoughtfully reexamine their prior assumptions about God and God's relationship with humanity. Are their beliefs consistent with a global understanding of the human situation as well as with the experiences of Jesus, the prophets, and the apostles? What does the Bible teach us about the cost of Christian discipleship? What are the important faith questions that arise when we face unexplained suffering?

Pastors and Christian leaders do a disservice to their members by preaching a theology of blessing that does not take into account the suffering and trauma that people experience. When facing adversity, those who suffer are sometimes criticized and blamed for their lack of faith. Too often they are encouraged to avoid questioning and simply praise the Lord in the midst of tragedy. Christians then mask their legitimate pain and sorrow rather than process it.

+ + +

I will never forget visiting the loud and lively Pentecostal worship service at a house church in Alabama twenty-five years ago. The pastor's wife, Ella, stood in front of the congregation sharing her testimony, punctuating her narrative with exclamations, "Praise the Lord! Praise Jesus! Praise the Lord!"

Ella's son died at the age of nineteen in a tragic automobile accident. The event occurred at least twenty years earlier. Before the congregation that Sunday morning, Ella recalled the moment when she received the phone call about her son's death. "I knew Satan wanted me to see this as a tragedy, but God wanted it to be a blessing. So I walked around my house and every time I nearly lost the victory, I shouted out, 'Praise the Lord! Praise the Lord!' It was hard to keep the victory, but whenever I faltered, I just praised Jesus," Ella testified.

My eyes were riveted on Ella's eyes as I watched pools of tears form in them and utterly refuse to fall down her ruddy cheeks. I listened to the quivering voice through which Ella proclaimed her triumphant story. As I sat captivated, I looked around me at all the nodding faces. I listened to the affirming Amen's of the gathered fellowship. Yet I was profoundly moved in a different way, it seemed, than all the rest.

This woman never let herself grieve for the loss of her son, I mused. *All these years have passed, and she still hasn't allowed herself to truly weep.* The tears that rimmed her eyes stayed fast in place. Glistening, they remained a haunting testimony to her grief, still intact, still untouched after twenty years of vigorous amen's and countless shouts of glorious praise.

Many people who cannot grieve in the church wind up leaving the church to do their grieving. If sorrow cannot be expressed and processed within the community of faith, it easily distills into depression or bitterness. Alienation from both God and the church can then result during times of such vulnerability and distress.

+ + +

Larry was a devout church-goer as a young child. He exhibited an unusual sensitivity to spiritual realities. During adolescence, his sister Geena was diagnosed with a rare and fatal disease that slowly robbed her of life. Geena endured a great deal of pain before she died.

Larry couldn't handle the pain of watching his beloved sister suffer. He couldn't understand why a loving God would not intervene and heal her. After Geena's funeral, Larry left the church, his simple, childlike faith shattered.

Thirty years later, Larry exhibited no interest in religious faith or practice. He felt that he had better things to do with his life than believe in "that God stuff," as he called it. His tragic story of unresolved grief and anger at God remained tucked in the recesses of his heart.

+ + +

It is critically important for Christians to address issues of suffering in ways that allow people to struggle with their faith in times of trial, but also to claim that same faith as a source of strength. Children are particularly vulnerable to intense disillusionment during times of suffering because their faith is so direct and their understanding so simple. Some have been intentionally sheltered from the roughness and tragedy of life. When sorrow visits them, they have no context for processing this universal reality.

Too often pastors offer shortsighted promises of blessing and prosperity for the faithful in all circumstances. The experience of suffering is not part of this theological equation. Many of our formulas about how God works do not hold up in times of crisis. Blaming the victim only deepens the sense of spiritual alienation that the suffering feel. Thus, facing inadequate theological assumptions becomes a critical issue for many of the dechurched.

Exploring each of these four areas—personal healing and recovery, systemic social issues, biblical interpretation, and theological understanding—is critical to the reconstruction of a damaged faith. All of these factors must be explored in order to rebuild a genuine and lasting relationship with God.

PART IV

How Can the Church Minister among the Dechurched?

CHAPTER 15

"God-Talk" and the Dechurched

In contemporary literature on evangelism and outreach, the needs of the dechurched are rarely distinguished from those of the unchurched. Yet the needs of these two groups couldn't be more different. The dechurched bring to renewed reflection on Christianity a slate that is full of past wounds and serious questions. This prior history with Christianity needs to be acknowledged and explored with openness and compassion. It frequently must be untangled on multiple levels—through pastoral care, biblical and theological reflection, and personal relationship.

The dechurched must never be treated as the objects of evangelistic techniques and programs. Personally, I don't believe anyone should be subjected to techniques when they replace genuine relationship. In the case of the dechurched, however, such treatment can cause even greater damage. An impersonal approach can reinforce attitudes about Christians already prevalent within the minds of those who have left the church: "These people care about my soul, but not about me," they complain.

During my first semester of graduate school in Alabama, I was extremely lonely. It was my first experience living in the deep South. I had never considered myself a Northerner before, but that was how others identified me at school. I thought the Civil War had ended one hundred years before, but people around me and even some local churches seemed caught up in the war as if it had happened yesterday. My fiancé was miles away in Indiana finishing his last semester of college. My piano professor had his favorite piano students whom he had taught since they were young. I was not only a newcomer to him but was also a Northerner in his mind. I lived in a predominantly freshman dorm that no longer housed a separate floor for graduate students. I liked going to bed early and being the first person to the music school in the morning; my roommate liked watching movies until 2 a.m. on her little television. I was miserable.

One day, a student stopped by my dormitory room and asked if she could share the Four Spiritual Laws with me. I was somewhat familiar with these evangelism materials. I told her that it wasn't necessary for her to review this pamphlet with me because I was already a Christian. She insisted, nonetheless, so I invited her to come in.

The student asked me, "Are you having any problems in your life right now?" I confessed to her that I felt very lonely and totally displaced. This stranger immediately pulled out her little blue pamphlet and began sharing with me how I could put Christ on the throne of my life and all my problems would disappear. I listened quietly to her presentation. She showed me a diagram of how one's life looked with the ego on the throne. She contrasted that with another diagram that showed how one's life was transformed when Christ was on the throne. She declared that Jesus Christ could dethrone all the difficulty and pain I was experiencing if I would truly trust him. Then she left, and I never saw her again.

This kind of evangelism may have satisfied some type of assignment to share "The Four Spiritual Laws" pamphlet with a certain number of students. Yet for me, it merely served to exacerbate my sense of alienation. I never forgot that experience. There I was, a Christian believer in a totally new environment, desperately needing friends. Along came this well-meaning student, offering me a formula of Christian spirituality that was supposed to make all my troubles disappear. I truly felt like an object of her evangelistic technique, not a person with feelings, concerns, and needs.

Even though I wasn't alienated from my faith at the time, I keenly sensed the irony of this experience. Dechurched people have their radar out to spot insincerity and ulterior motives among Christians. Many have already experienced insensitivity or hypocrisy among those who once acted like friends or mentors. The best thing a person reaching out to such individuals can do is to set aside all the techniques found in evangelism books or church growth seminars and seek to be a genuine and caring friend. Before reengaging in the faith themselves, the dechurched need extended opportunities to observe Christians once again. Forcing conversations about God while building trust often causes the dechurched to distance themselves further from Christians. Sometimes it is critical not to talk about the faith, but to show forth the love of Christ in simple yet meaningful ways.

Another significant aspect of outreach among the dechurched is an awareness of the impact created by the use of particular language about God. Christian groups have their own distinctive ways of talking about the faith. Along with other phrases, terms like *born-again*, *saved*, *witnessing*, and *soul winning* all have their own meanings within various churches and faith traditions. Some Christians pepper their conversations with exclamations such as "Praise the Lord!" or "Thanks be to God!" For those who have been excluded or hurt by the church, certain words or phrases may trigger intense reactions to past experiences.

+ + +

Gloria recounted a conversation she had as a new Christian while attending a college fellowship group. A science major, Gloria was trying to reconcile the biblical accounts of creation in Genesis 1—2 with her long-held belief in evolution. Innocently, Gloria mentioned to the other students some thoughts she had about the first few chapters of Genesis. Rather than help Gloria struggle with her questions about faith and science, the students quickly jumped on Gloria for harboring any doubts about a literal interpretation of creationism. They told Gloria that she couldn't genuinely be born-again if she had any misgivings about creationism as her Christian peers interpreted its doctrines.

Gloria was thrown into a period of self-doubt about the validity of her recent conversion. Years later, she can recount this story easily, but Gloria still cannot hear the phrase *born-again* without remembering the intensity of pain, exclusion, and judgment that she felt twenty years before at a time when she was vulnerable and hungering to grow in her newfound faith.

+ + +

In my years as a Baptist pastor, I have discovered that the word *Baptist* is a trigger word in the lives of many dechurched Baptists. Most of them were raised in homes and churches where questioning was not permitted. As adults, anytime they encountered another Baptist (something they generally tried to avoid) either consciously or unconsciously, all their negative associations with the word *Baptist* came to mind. Even non-Baptists often have striking stereotypes and fears about Baptists. Over and over, people who have finally made a home at The First Baptist Church of Oberlin have said, "I visited nearly every church in town, but I could never picture myself setting foot in a *Baptist* church."

Frequently, individuals who have experienced sexual abuse or emotional neglect by a father or father figure have great difficulty relating to the Father imagery many churches use exclusively for God. Among these people, the image of "Father" is not a welcoming one. Instead, it is a word associated with feelings of rejection and betrayal. Such reactions may be so intense and unconscious that the person struggling with them has no idea why she or he feels so excluded by predominantly male imagery and language about God.

+ + +

Olivia, a preacher's daughter, shared her struggles very candidly on this as she reached young adulthood: "My father was cold and emotionally unavailable. He was always away 'doing the Lord's work.' He was very inattentive to the needs of our family. When I hear God referred to as my Father, I feel nothing but distance. I have had to envision God with different words, in different ways, to be able to understand God as loving and nurturing."

+ + +

For ten years, my husband worked as a chaplain in a countywide youth detention facility. In this capacity, he led weekly Bible studies with interested youth. One day as he described the nature of God's love to the incarcerated girls, he asked them, "Who in your lives most resembles this God I have described to you?"

Without hesitation, the majority of the girls present chose their grandmothers. These women loved their errant granddaughters no matter what the girls did. They always had an encouraging word or helpful suggestion to share. They prayed for their granddaughters in spite of disappointment after disappointment. The grandmothers didn't give up on these adolescents even when many others had.

A significant number of the girls in the detention home had been deserted or abused by the males in their lives. Fathers and stepfathers had used them; boyfriends had beaten them; brothers had fought with them. Their experiences of men rarely included positive role models of nurture, caring, and comfort. Yet their grandmothers were different.

There was little hope of communicating the love of God to these girls if it was described as the love of a Father, even a caring Father. Such a concept was out of reach to them. These teenagers could, however, imagine a loving God if that God cared about them as much as their grandmothers did.

+ + +

Imagery that pushes some away from God at times helps others rediscover important truths about God and themselves. I have often led women's study groups at other churches. I met Betty at one such event. Her father had been an alcoholic as long as she could remember. He was never there for her during the most important moments of her life. Betty confessed to me, "It may seem strange, but embracing God as a loving father has helped me accept the miserable relationship I had with my human father. I never had an earthly father who loved me unconditionally. To understand God as a father with an unending commitment to my well-being has allowed me to begin healing the father wound in my life."

+ + +

The Bible is filled with rich and diverse imagery about God. Moses experienced God in the midst of a burning bush and as a cloud by day and a pillar of fire by night (Exodus 3:1–6; 13:21–22).

The saints of ancient times knew many names for God: *Elohim, Yahweh,* and *El Shaddai* among them. God is compared in scripture to a mother eagle tending her young (Deuteronomy 32:11–12), a nursing mother (Isaiah 49:15), and a generous father (Matthew 7:7–11). God is described as a fortress and rock (Psalm 18:2; 31:3; 71:3), a refuge (Psalm 91:2), and a shelter (Psalm 61:3). Christ compares his ministry to that of a good shepherd (John 10:1–16), a mother hen longing to gather her brood under her wings (Matthew 23:37), a woman searching for a lost coin (Luke 15:8–10), a patient father yearning for his wayward son to return home (Luke 15:11–32), and a bridegroom longing to be wholly united to his bride (Mark 2:19–20; John 3:29; Revelation 19:5–9). The Holy Spirit is understood as a comforter, advocate, and instrument of truth and righteousness (John 15:26—16:15). The Spirit acts as a divine birthing agent (Luke 1:35; John 3:8). The language used to describe the power, majesty, tenderness, commitment, mercy, care, and love of the Holy One supersedes even our loftiest human descriptions of the Divine. The church that wishes to minister among the dechurched will make good use of the numerous images scripture offers as we seek to know God.

In the lives of the dechurched, issues of language become either bridges or barriers to hearing the larger truth of the gospel of Jesus Christ. It is critical to provide opportunities to explore faith issues by using vocabularies that do not trigger past experiences of alienation or abuse. When intense reactions unavoidably occur, these feelings must be acknowledged, named, and examined. Otherwise, the possibility of healing and renewed faith remains hopelessly blocked and mired in past hurts.

There are many ways to describe biblical concepts. A church can develop a rich language of faith, even without the constant use of traditional words for that faith. Retaining the meaning of a biblical concept is the critical element in its translation. Phrases such as "being made new," "being renewed," or "giving one's life to Christ" express the idea of transformation inherent in the popular phrase "born-again." "Witnessing" can also be described by such phrases as "sharing the faith" or "telling the faith story." The concept of "church growth" can be spoken about using language such as "outreach" or "becoming an inviting church." "Salvation" can be described in terms of reconciliation with God or choosing to follow Christ. "Sin" can be understood by words and phrases such as "brokenness," "missing the mark," or "being alienated from God." As the meanings of these theological terms are fleshed out and explained, it is possible to help people hear the gospel message anew. As the dechurched begin reclaiming the substance of their faith, the discovery of words to explain their experiences with God will become part of their healing processes. The language of faith that is developed will reflect a new expression of reality as well as profound truths about God and about themselves.

As time passes, it may be possible for those who are reconstructing their faith to gain insight into the impact of language, past or present, as it helps or hinders their journey. If the church is ever going to move forward with its own ministry, this must happen. For years at The First Baptist Church of Oberlin, certain concepts elicited strong reactions from the formerly dechurched. One of these was church growth.

Pastors know that no church can survive for long without facing the issue of church growth. How does a pastor deal with Rick and Nancy's powerful reactions to past experiences in a large, impersonal congregation that was driven by attendance goals? How does one speak to the rejection that Sally felt when another Christian told her she wasn't a true believer because she was struggling with certain scriptures? How does one address Roger's pain over the years of judgment his sister heaped on him when he wasn't active in any church? All of these issues might never surface when the phrase "church growth" is used, but they simmer underneath the dialogue and impact a congregation's ability to move forward in the area of outreach.

Two ways to deal with this problem are helpful. One is to use many different words to embody the concept of church growth. At First Baptist Church, we talk about outreach rather than church growth. The term *outreach* has a broader and richer meaning for the congregation than merely padding the numbers in our own pews. Further, it affirms the many ways that church members minister within the community, even when their efforts do not lead to the actual numerical growth of the congregation itself. Outreach embodies acts of mercy, charity, and kindness. Outreach includes both speaking and doing. To the members of First Baptist, the concept of outreach remains untainted from ulterior motives. The concept of church growth does not. Are we reaching out to people because it is part of being Christian, or are we doing it just so we can get more people in our own doors? These are important issues of theology and ministry for members of our congregations.

Another critical way we deal with this problem of language around church growth is to talk about our various reactions to the concept of church growth itself. This way, we can begin to uncover those silent stories of the heart that rumble around without resolution. "I remember being newcomers in our previous community and having two men from an area church visit my husband and me," Nancy comments. "They told us all about their church and ended their little talk by saying, 'We are having a church growth contest to see if we can top 500 in our church school. If you both come, we will reach 457.' That completely turned me off. I felt like a number, some numerical goal, not a person with gifts to offer."

Roger compares his story to Nancy's by saying, "My brother Don became a Christian before I did. Every time I saw him, all he cared about was my soul. He never wanted to know about my job, my kids, my problems, my joys. It was a long time before I was able to think about God for myself, because I became allergic to any talk about religion after a while."

As people open up, they can deal together with their reactions to various types of church language. This allows them to discover healthy and honest ways to explore the issues at hand. This benefits the whole faith community while maintaining the integrity of the community's witness.

Another trigger phrase at First Baptist Church is "business meeting." For years, the majority of the congregation has harbored an intense disdain for structure. The formerly dechurched among us rarely wanted to participate in committees or planning meetings. Some had come from churches where multiple layers of organization obscured the more important tasks of ministry. Some left communities where petty issues dominated the discussion. Parishioners at First Baptist expressed a longing for creativity and variety rather than a yearning for the routine and familiar.

Steve and I struggled perpetually with how to address the issue of structure and the necessity for business meetings. We continued the inherited structure of quarterly meetings held in the evening followed by a big annual meeting in January. Yet few people would show up at these important gatherings where we addressed critical issues of ministry, church maintenance, and community envisioning. We tried all kinds of ways to make these events interesting. One spring, I developed a humorous quiz with true and false questions about the church's finances in order to help people realize what they actually did and didn't know regarding the monetary situation of the church. No matter what we tried, attendance at business meetings was always minimal.

After graduation, an Oberlin College alumna from First Baptist became actively involved in the Church of the Savior in Washington, D.C. Janey was so enthusiastic about her new church home that she often wrote to me about the life and organization of the congregation. She even sent me a few books about the church. As I began reading about The Church of the Savior's attempts at community organization, a whole new vision of church structure began dawning on me. *We are such a small congregation, the whole church community could really be "the Board,"* I mused. *What if we had monthly community meetings right after church where we explored various issues of relevance to the congregation and dispensed with quarterly business meetings entirely? What if we developed ad hoc ministry teams around specific needs and did away with our two traditional boards?*

The idea seemed perfect in many ways. Parishioners didn't have to attend an extra night meeting since they would already be at church. We could literally "tuck in" the issues of boiler replacement, sidewalk repair, or special offerings among planning the church Thanksgiving dinner or supporting a family facing serious illness. We could articulate these seemingly mundane issues within the context of building community life rather than doing church business.

For the past several years, our community meetings have been a wonderful success. The attendance has frequently been triple what we once had at quarterly and annual business meetings. Transforming dry business meetings into engaging community meetings has been a step toward awakening the energies of the entire congregation.

Many churches are highly resistant to changes such as those that I have suggested. The idea of expanding their vocabulary for both God and the basic tenets of their faith is met with accusations of diluting the gospel. The thought of experimenting with new structures that may release pent-up creativity and hidden talents is considered unconscionable. "If it was good enough for the church I grew up in, it's good enough for the church today," such critics complain.

I would hazard a guess that congregations resistant to any expansion of language or change in structure are not eager to respond to the issues the dechurched may face as they consider reentering the life of faith or the world of the church. If dechurched people are going to return to the fold, they will often talk about God in different ways than they may have in the past. The verbalization and understanding of their faith will be nuanced in ways that it previously was not. Their approach to doing ministry and being involved in the church may also be transformed. Our congregations must be ready to structure themselves in fresh ways, or they will never begin to speak to the needs of this population.

CHAPTER 16

Creating a Church for the Dechurched

If the dechurched come to the point of giving the church another chance, they are nearly always determined to "do church" in a different way. For them, church cannot be content in offering a shallow theology replete with pat answers. Church cannot be more committed to numerical growth than to the people it seeks to reach. Church cannot be exclusive or arrogant about its own understanding of the truth. Church cannot be insensitive to the pains and needs of the world. Church cannot be superficial or uncomfortable in dealing with the struggles of its members. Church cannot expect to produce automatic saints. Church cannot reject people who are different or who stumble frequently while seeking to follow Christ. Church cannot ignore the trauma of mental illness as it impacts members or their families. Church cannot be preoccupied with money, the color of the next carpet, where the choir stands, or the design for the prayer room. On and on the list goes.

The dechurched often have a clearer sense of what they do not want the church to be like than what they actually want or need in congregational life. The dechurched often harbor within themselves a profound sense of what a church should be, but that awareness is obscured by intense reactions to what the church has been in their experience. Thus, a positive vision may be very difficult to call forth at first.

+ + +

I will never forget the comments of Marlene, a strong lay leader in an inner-city church with a powerful ministry to the dechurched. Her tiny congregation of thirty members reaches out daily to immigrants, the homeless, the homosexual community, the mentally ill, and the poor. For the first few years of the church's outreach in the city, its members sought to describe its identity to outsiders using the language of "church family." *Visit our church and experience the family of God in action!* the church's publicity stated. Before long, however, the congregation discovered that people were coming to the church and quickly feeling disillusioned by their engagement with the very people who reached out to them. It wasn't that the church folks were bad people, or insincere people, or even gossipy people—they were just real people with real struggles and, at times, real differences of opinion.

The church members began to realize that many of the newcomers had been alienated from their families, rejected by their loved ones, or displaced from their cultures and countries. Their inner-city neighborhoods were racked with violence, poverty, and indifference. For years, many of them had been fending for themselves, finding few others along the journey whom they could truly trust. In fact, most of the newcomers held on to highly unrealistic and idealistic concepts of family. They thought that this church family was going to be all that their own families and neighborhoods had never been. Everyone would always get along. No one would argue or disagree. There would be no personality conflicts, no difficulties having their needs met. The problems of life would disappear in the idyllic rush of friendship, caring, and resourcefulness that this new church family would provide.

The idealism about healthy families that these newcomers possessed was getting them into trouble. The old-timers knew that the newcomers could indeed discover church family in their midst. However, church family would not be perfect and also could not erase the deficit of love many of these folks had experienced in the past.

Newcomers needed to see that even church families faced conflict. Yet disagreements among these Christians weren't resolved through violence, threat, or intimidation. Healthy church families included diverse personalities that at times clashed, but everyone was nonetheless appreciated and affirmed. Church families were those who received help and experienced redemption amid their many weaknesses, frailties, and differences.

This inner-city church decided that it was time to alter its paradigm for community life. Whenever the congregation used the language of church family in its literature, explanations were included describing what, in fact, church family was and what it was not.

+ + +

It is difficult to work with the core issues of the church when they become trigger issues that surface past injuries members have faced. Trigger areas may be as varied as church growth, stewardship, evangelism, or community building. Such topics are essential aspects of church life. Finding a way to talk about them sincerely, without the discussion flattening into diffuse reactions to prior experiences, is a challenge for anyone pastoring a church open to the needs of the dechurched.

A Church for the Dechurched may need to approach evangelism from the standpoint of personal testimony rather than programmed techniques and prepared approaches. Discussions of stewardship will have to be tempered by reassurances that the church is ministry driven, not financially driven. Reminders that it takes money to maintain many types of ministry will need to be verbalized. Reflections around the topic of church growth may require delving into the actual meaning and motivation for ministry that ultimately is not growth of our particular church over that of others, as much as we may desire that growth. Our purpose is to bear witness to the reign of God, to demonstrate and share our faith through our words and deeds. The fruit of such efforts that falls in our direction is simply an added blessing.

A few years ago, I had lunch with one of our parishioners to share ideas about church ministry. Virginia is a very artistic, creative, and thoughtful woman. She was well acquainted with the lack of relationship at times between the ministry the church offered and the numbers of people who participated in the life of the congregation. As we talked, Virginia was eager to share a recent insight with me. At its core was a vision of an enormous tree, replete with greenery and ripe with luscious fruit. What a glorious image! The tree was deeply rooted in the middle of the sanctuary of First Baptist Church. The branches were willowy and extended. They stretched out beyond the beautiful stained-glass windows of the church and bore much fruit that fell outside those same windows.

This image described more than a thousand words could explain. Indeed, it was a profound snapshot of the ministry of the church. The roots of the church's work among the dechurched grew deeply in the soil of the sanctuary, in our close relationships with one another in the pews. The church's ministry sprouted richly from events as commonplace as the camaraderie of church cleanup days, singing in the choir, praying for one another, studying the Bible together, or sharing in fellowship dinners. Many of those grafted on to the tree growing within the sanctuary were themselves once among the ranks of the dechurched.

The tree bore its fruit, some falling within the church and maturing until fully ripened. Time and time again, the fruit also fell outside the windows of our little church. Many touched by the life of the church never entered its doors or participated in its community life. The branches of the tree that stretched outside the church's windows continued bearing fruit in their own time. The image was beautiful to envision, and the whole tree was the work of God.

I was reminded how necessary it is to constantly look beyond the mundane yet quantifiable issues of weekly church attendance, quarterly budgets, and denominational statistics to grasp the ministry we share together as a congregation. The vision that God gave Virginia has stayed with me and provided a profound sense of encouragement time and time again.

The relationship between ministry to the dechurched and the numbers of church attenders in the pew is unpredictable and tenuous. If there is anything I have learned in twenty years of ministry among this population, it is this fact of life. I recently spoke with a group of area pastors about the needs of the dechurched, the importance of distinguishing them from the unchurched, and the challenges they offer the church. One pastor spoke up, saying, "I guess our church doesn't really think about these people because we consider them beyond repentance if they have already rejected a faith they once professed. Besides, it seems a lot easier to reach the unchurched than the dechurched."

The church that desires a large following, flashy results, or rapid numerical growth had better look elsewhere for a new ministry than among the dechurched. Working with this population is not an easy calling. Trust between active Christians and those who have left the church and/or their faith is built slowly, over time. Many twists, turns, and setbacks occur along the way. Churches and denominations that commit themselves to ministry among this population need to be sensitive to the complexities that accompany their efforts.

+ + +

Troy and Ellen were new church planters. They were doing some of the most innovative, exciting ministry that I had witnessed in a long time. Their new church plant was in an area where a very large congregation had split apart after several months of infighting and dissension. Nearly half the membership had left. Lingering conflicts and strong feelings of betrayal remained among the dechurched from this congregation. Some of these people began attending the new church plant that Troy and Ellen were nurturing.

Troy and Ellen were feeling pressured by their denominational leadership to meet specific goals for church growth and financial viability within their new church plant. These goals were placed on a timetable that this couple became increasingly convinced the church could not meet. Yet there was an undeniable need for their ministry in the neighborhood where they had been placed.

Ellen attended several workshops I offered on ministry among the dechurched. As I reached the point of explaining the frequent lack of relationship between enhanced denominational statistics and ministry among the dechurched, Ellen stopped me. "This is our problem," she said with a sense of conviction in her voice. "This is it! So many of the people we are reaching are coming from difficult church situations that they left feeling greatly distressed. We are doing extensive pastoral counseling with these people. We are unable to focus on the issues of numbers and money to the extent that is expected."

I counseled Ellen to speak with Troy about the special challenges of working among the dechurched. I also encouraged the two of them to approach their denominational leadership together and explain the nature of their particular work in church planting. They could illuminate some of the differences between working among the dechurched and reaching out to the unchurched. Presenting a solid rationale for extended deadlines, they could argue for flexibility in approaching the specific realities of their own ministry context. The last time I saw them, they remained joyously immersed in the life and ministry of their new church plant. From this encounter, I assumed that they were able to navigate their particular challenges in a positive way.

+ + +

A Church for the Dechurched thirsts for fresh paradigms in being the church. One such model that has been helpful to me is that of the circuit-riding church. Decades ago, pastors in North America traveled from village to village ministering to people in different houses of worship. The circuit-riding church is a variation of this pattern. Instead of moving from place to place, the pastor among the dechurched discovers that his or her "charges" are uniquely scattered. They come from many denominations. Their life stories are incredibly diverse. They may be neighbors, relatives, coworkers, or even former church members. They may show up for support groups or social events. They may be spouses of parishioners. They may be members of an alienated social group. They may want little to do with Christians and nothing to do with churches for years, but then one day they may show up at a Christmas pageant or church picnic. Many within the circuit of the church never wind up in the pews of the very churches that reach out to them.

During the early years my husband and I spent in Oberlin, several people came to First Baptist Church during a time of major personal crisis. Some faced difficult family situations as children reached their teen years and rejected parental authority. Others were adjusting to life after a divorce or the death of a family member. Some experienced the displacement created by picking up roots and relocating for new jobs. A number came after either leaving other churches or being disengaged from any faith community for many years.

Steve and I plunged into the challenges of providing ministry to this diverse population. Frequently, we found that an individual or family left First Baptist after their crisis was either partially resolved or some healing had begun. I struggled with this pattern of coming, receiving, and leaving. I could not understand it. Why would a person leave a church after encountering such a loving and compassionate touch during a time of great vulnerability and need? This reality felt at times like a rejection of the ministry we were providing.

Eventually, it occurred to me that this pattern might be a coping mechanism among people yearning to start over. This leads me to the second model of The Church for the Dechurched, which I have witnessed in action: the intensive care unit. The First Baptist Church of Oberlin has frequently functioned as such a space. People in all manner of pain come into the church community where they can just "be" until the healing springs water the soul, life is restored to a place of greater stability, and the future becomes hopeful once again.

An intensive care unit, however, is never meant to become a permanent home. A time of transition inevitably arises. We all hope to eventually leave our periods of weakness behind. A significant number of people have been able to make this journey from brokenness to renewal while remaining in the congregation. The church that has anchored their lives during difficult times continues to feed and nourish their souls. Others feel the need to change the scenery and leave the past behind. For these, remaining in the church that bound up their wounds becomes a persistent reminder of their former brokenness.

This variety of reactions can be compared to the decision making that a person experiences after a loved one dies. Some carefully preserve the room of the deceased, hallowing the space and the memories attached to it, retaining everything just as it was when the person was alive. Others find they cannot adequately move on unless they change nearly everything. They clean out the treasured belongings and save only the most precious items. They relocate to new homes or towns, closer to family members or farther away. They take new jobs or embark on new adventures. They explore interests that have been submerged for decades.

People transition from the intensive care unit to the rest of life in diverse ways. A brief period of intense ministry is never offered in vain. It is a critical link on the road toward healing.

+ + +

Oftentimes, First Baptist Church attracts the dechurched from other denominations. A significant number return to their denominational roots after a season at our church. A Baptist church at times is a radical departure from the styles of worship familiar to such individuals. The church provides a way station where they can reflect on what they value from their past. People can sort out their disagreements with the tradition in which they were reared. They can discover anew what is truly important to them within their unique histories of faith.

Nina and Rod attended First Baptist with their two small children. Nina had grown up in the Catholic church but had been away from it for a long time. Rod was raised in a different Christian tradition. For a year, this family participated actively in worship and fellowship activities at the church.

One day Nina came to my husband and me, saying, "It has been a wonderful experience to be here at this church. I have treasured the spiritual depth of this congregation, and people have received our family so warmly. We have decided to go back to the Catholic church now. Being here has helped me realize what I love about the church of my childhood. I miss celebrating the eucharist every Sunday as I did in the Catholic church. I miss the rituals and liturgies that undergirded my life long ago. I will always be thankful for our year here, but it is time for us to move on."

Nina and her family returned to the church tradition that felt like home. To this day, they are active members of a local Catholic church. The year that they spent in an entirely different spiritual setting helped them to reevaluate their own traditions and gain a richer, deeper knowledge of what the past truly meant to them and what they needed for the years to come.

+ + +

All of these experiences taught me valuable lessons about working with the dechurched. For many, periods of transition from one way of being to another were critical opportunities for growth. These included processing difficult situations from the past, stepping back from denominational roots while sorting out their personal meaning, or navigating presenting crises and their many implications within one's life. Some who find a safe spiritual environment in the church to tackle this inner work will eventually make that place their spiritual home. A significant number will not. Both encompass aspects of the church's ministry among the dechurched.

+ + +

I always wished that Reta had visited First Baptist Church before she graduated from Oberlin College. A second-generation child of dechurched parents, she had never been inside a church or attended any kind of church function in her twenty-two years of life. Involvement in a twelve-step program opened her up to the concept of a higher power. During her senior year of college, her curiosity about Christianity became more insistent, and she began attending a discussion group on campus led by Christians.

As Reta approached her graduation date, I wanted so much to share my life as a copastor of First Baptist Church with her. I wanted Reta to meet the wonderful people in the congregation and experience the warmth and genuineness of our worship services. I wanted the opportunity to help break down some of the generational taboos against church that were part of Reta's history.

I invited Reta to come to church the last Sunday before graduation. She said, "Oh, I don't want to do that. You all will be singing songs I don't know. You will be standing up and sitting down when I'm not sure what to do. I just don't think I'd be comfortable in a church service yet."

People like Reta become part of the circuit of the church ministering among the first- or second-generation dechurched. While the impact of Christians who accompany them on the journey to faith can never be measured by statistics or quantified in professional reports, the angels in heaven rejoice over each lost one who is found.

+ + +

The church ministering among the dechurched must consider the number of lives it impacts, not by counting heads in the pews, but by exploring the breadth of the circuit of the church. Who is part of that larger circuit? What about Kathie, the remarried neighbor who no longer feels comfortable in her own church because her divorce fifteen years ago was never recognized? What about George, the ex-Baptist who was thrown out of his church for being gay? What about Richard who pastored a Pentecostal church for decades until his church rejected him for supporting his only son, who died of AIDS? What about Kevin, who lost his job after his pastor encouraged him to quit taking the medication that helped him gain control over chronic mental illness? What about Deborah, who as a child lost her mother to cancer and hasn't forgiven God after two decades? All around us we discover the dechurched with their own private pains, stories, and struggles.

The process of believing again can take months and even years. It is not uncommon for a friendship with a dechurched person to develop for two or three years before it leads to any significant conversation on spiritual issues. Those who shape the Church for the Dechurched must constantly remember that it is God who transforms others, not ourselves. We may plant many seeds and reap only a few harvests. Healing from spiritual trauma, abuse, addiction, tragedy, or any other hurt is a slow process in any human life. Insight and transformation are rarely immediate. Rather, deepening circles of awareness occur as periods of fallowness frequently alternate with periods of activity.

+ + +

One of my most memorable stories about the slow process of rediscovering faith is that of Belinda. I met this woman two decades ago while visiting new residents in town. Unlike many others, Belinda was eager to invite a Baptist stranger into her home and share bits of her story. As I sat and talked with her, she spoke eagerly about her Baptist roots. She recounted many of the challenges and heartaches in her life and recalled long periods when she had turned her back on God. As Belinda and I become friends, she divulged many of the tragedies and addictions of her life—a family history of incest and physical abuse, years living as a prostitute on city streets, an abortion secretly paid for by a pastor who tried in vain to reach her.

Somewhere in Belinda's heart she yearned to be close to God. We began studying the Bible together. I made an agreement with Belinda that I would explore the scriptures with her as long as she desired to do so, with only one stipulation: she had to take the time to read each passage for herself before we got together to discuss it. Belinda welcomed this opportunity at first, but eventually squeezed our meetings in between alcoholic binges and one-night stands with men she befriended after work at bars.

As time passed, Belinda became less engaged in our Bible study and more caught up in her drinking and anonymous sexual encounters. One day she even said to me, "When my life ends, I wonder if the book written about me will be a triumphant testimony of Christian faith or *The Story of the Happy Hooker!*"

Time passed and nothing changed. Belinda came to Bible study unprepared, flitted through our discussion, and frequented an area bar afterward. After much soul-searching, I finally called her and said that I would no longer continue studying the scriptures with her unless she kept her part of the agreement—reading the text ahead of time. Belinda was outraged that I held her to this. She lectured me on the phone saying, "What kind of Christian are you, anyway, that you won't do a Bible study with me unless I read the material first? I thought Christians were supposed to love people unconditionally!" She hung up.

Our conversation was among the more difficult ones I have had during my years in ministry. After talking with Belinda, I agonized over the decision I had made. Had I expected too much? Had I loved too little? Was I shutting off the one link Belinda had to a faith she held dear years before as a small child? I was unsure of the answers to these questions.

Our lives drifted apart without the weekly Bible studies that once connected us, but I kept praying for Belinda. Beneath all the problems of her life, I could still see a tender heart hungering to leave her addictions behind and reclaim her identity as a child of God.

A few years passed. One day Belinda called me to tell me she had nearly lost her job. She wanted to let me know that she had prayed about what to do and listened to the answer she received in prayer. Even though other employees were released, the situation turned out to her advantage. "Can you believe that God still hears my prayers?" she asked me incredulously, with a tone of hopefulness in her voice.

More years passed, and my contact with Belinda became increasingly rare. One day she called from an inpatient drug treatment program. After receiving three drunken driving citations, Belinda had been court-ordered to attend the program. During her hospitalization, she was expected to participate in Alcoholics Anonymous. She had reached the point in the twelve-step program where she needed to share her confession with someone. She wanted that confidante to be me. I drove many miles to be present with her and listen to her life story, recounted in more detail than I had ever heard it told before. At long last Belinda was forced to face the consequences of her choices. She was afraid that this time she really would lose her job. I hoped, once again, for transformation in her life, whether she lost her job or not.

I continued praying for Belinda. In the many years I had known her, Belinda had tried church off and on, but never The First Baptist Church of Oberlin. She had an attraction to churches whose dynamics resembled those of the dysfunctional family in which she was raised. She wanted to be yelled at and scolded by the preacher. She yearned for noise and emotion. She savored ecstatic feelings of release. And then she wanted to repeat this cycle all over again the following Sunday.

When Belinda did visit churches, she often became involved in the place, conflicts and scandals arose, and she left. In one church, she became sexually involved with a church leader. I never saw her seek a place of worship healthy enough to help her face and overcome her deep personal problems. She kept her struggles carefully hidden or acted them out and then disappeared.

Belinda's employer transferred her out of Ohio. Again, I didn't hear from Belinda for a long time. At least ten years after we first met, there was a little note attached to the door of the church office. Belinda had come back to town and looked for me. She hadn't found me, but she left a message saying, "Guess what? I'm getting my life together and feel good about it. For the first time in years, I'm involved in a church that is a healthy place for me. You would be proud of me. I recommitted my life to Christ. I don't think the final chapter of my life will be *The Happy Hooker* after all. I just wanted you to know."

+ + +

A Church for the Dechurched must fully embrace its seed-planting ministry. Even when the dechurched never attend a particular church whose members touch their lives, they often look to the place and the people in the congregation as a valuable testimony, inspiration, and example. Two college students, one of whom I have never met, sent my husband and me electronic mail messages expressing their gratitude for the presence of The First Baptist Church in Oberlin. Both students said, "It gives me hope to know there are genuine Christians out there." One student confessed that she was finally able to call herself a Christian again after several years of disassociating herself from the faith of her childhood.

My husband once offered a study group called "How Can I Believe Again?" He designed provocative posters that included a person scaling a high fence topped with barbed wire. The flyer summarized the variety of topics to be explored. Steve and I prayed that this group would provide a needed outreach to the dechurched within the wider Oberlin community. When the first meeting took place, only two people came, both of whom were members of First Baptist Church interested in hearing the stories of others who might attend. No actively dechurched people attended any session. We were deeply disappointed by this lack of response. We had prayed so much. We had sought God's direction in designing the topics for group exploration. What had gone wrong?

In conversations around town, I discovered that the flyers had piqued significant thought and discussion. One woman sought me out at a community event. "I saw the flyers about that study group, 'How Can I Believe Again?'" she said. "I'm so mixed up in my beliefs, I really should come." She chronicled half a dozen denominations plus several New Age groups that she had dabbled in over the years. It was obvious that she had many spiritual issues roaming her heart, but she never attended.

Another woman, whose daughter had attempted suicide, confided in a church member saying, "I really need something like that group, but my journey has been just too painful to talk about. I don't think I'm ready to face my spiritual questions."

In this instance, the ministry to the dechurched turned out to be the flyers about the study group, not the meetings themselves. These posters seemed to pry a few hearts open a little bit, though not enough to risk participation in a group setting. Through this experience, I realized that ministry among the dechurched encounters much deeper resistance than I ever imagined.

The Church for the Dechurched will never look like a traditional church. It simply can't. The impact of those reentering congregational life must be felt in the way a congregation "does church." Creativity must be nurtured. Questions—of any and all kinds—must be valued and welcomed. Doubt must be allowed as it paves the way for fragile faith. Pain must be honestly acknowledged and accepted as a reality of life.

The dechurched will never bring to the church neat, packaged, orthodox theology. Folks like that tend to be the "churched," not the dechurched. Oftentimes, the theology of the dechurched reflects a reaction to their pain more than an affirmation of their beliefs. If they have to have their theology all worked out before they can participate in the church, they won't ever do it. They have lived without the approval or blessing of the church in the past. To continue to do so is no challenge for them. A Church for the Dechurched has to accept the faith journey as a *journey,* not a predetermined destination. People will grow toward Christ if given the opportunity for long-term acceptance, nurture, and support. It may be a bumpy ride, and it won't look exactly alike for any two people; but, if the hunger is there, the growth will come, and the church will be blessed along the way.

CHAPTER 17

Accompanying the Dechurched

To accompany the dechurched on the journey toward wholeness requires great patience. It can be a painful process for those who remain in the faith. Regardless of the challenges and roadblocks that are strewn along the pathway, there is great rejoicing when the person living in doubt or disbelief discovers renewed faith, when the broken person finds healing and release.

My experience with this population, while valid, is certainly limited. Further, those whom I have personally encountered could not possibly adequately represent the dechurched among all races, classes, personalities, and even theological perspectives within the Christian faith. Yet I hope that readers can take from my own experience some insights that transcend the particular and provide encouragement as they face their own unique contexts for ministry.

Throughout this chapter, I will use the phrase "companion of the dechurched" to describe the one who ministers among the dechurched. I choose this phrase for many reasons. While pastors as well as counselors may offer directed spiritual care to such individuals, professionals are certainly not the only ones who labor among this group. Friends, neighbors, and relatives all participate in this journey as well.

Good listening skills are an indispensable resource for working among the dechurched. Reaching out means saying, "Hello, how are you?" time and time again to someone who is openly unfriendly and seemingly uninterested in talking to a Christian. Reaching out requires being attentive to difficult stories, even when they are filled with pain, anger, and profound disillusionment. Reaching out means refraining from offering quick answers, choosing instead to provide friendship and encouragement.

A person eager to help a dechurched friend or family member will play a critical role as a listener. The dechurched usually have had enough of talkers who tell them what to believe, how to believe, what to do, and how to do it. They need to reclaim their own voices in the life of faith and forge their own pathways toward God.

Anyone working among this population must respect the inviolability of the stories shared with them. We cannot argue with the experience of others. We may find their testimonies tragic and disturbing. We may be appalled or grieved by them. We may disagree with how the dechurched have interpreted their life experiences or how they have navigated painful episodes. Had we walked in the shoes of our dechurched friends or neighbors, we might have responded differently. Regardless of all our reactions to the lives and testimonies of the dechurched, a person's experience *just is,* and it must first be respected in order for it to be taken seriously. A friend of the dechurched cannot become a vehicle of redemption and healing without embracing the other's story in the totality of how she or he has known it. Every experience that causes one to lose faith must be treated with incredible gentleness and respect. It must be regarded as the tragedy that it was felt as.

Loving the dechurched may mean asking thoughtful, clarifying questions that can help the person explore his or her own inner terrain. Sometimes it is critical to withhold the answers we ourselves have discovered or at least wait to share our own perspectives until we have invited the dechurched person to speak.

+ + +

Rebecca was deeply wounded by a Christian friend she once trusted without question. The situation escalated, and others whom Rebecca hardly knew became involved. After nearly two years, no resolution of the relationship was in sight. Rebecca faced periods of depression and attacks of anxiety in the wake of these incidents.

One night Rebecca called me on the phone to share how she was doing. She sought information from me about Christian events on campus. As I responded, she exploded with expletives and bursts of anger. The conversation felt like a war zone laced with land mines. I wasn't sure which direction it would take from minute to minute. I had no idea what fury my words might trigger.

I wanted to help Rebecca listen to herself. I decided to take a direct approach and said, "Tell me, Rebecca, what does swearing do for you?"

Rebecca paused for a moment. The brief silence was refreshing to me after her sharp outbursts. She finally commented, "I swear a lot these days, Mary. Somehow it is a way of rebelling against just 'being nice' and acting like nothing has happened. It is a way of acknowledging my anger, I guess." After another moment of silence, Rebecca then asked me, "Do you understand what I mean?"

My initial question provided Rebecca with the opportunity to reflect on the way her unresolved issues in one relationship spilled over into other relationships, particularly into her phone conversation with me. Had I simply criticized Rebecca for the way she chose to express her feelings, she would have left the conversation with a verbal hand slap but no new insight about herself. Had I simply ignored my own reactions to what was happening, I would have left Rebecca with no truthful exchange between the two of us. Had I chosen to share a scripture verse or two about the power of the tongue, I am certain that my comments would only have driven Rebecca farther away from me and perhaps from God.

. At this point, Rebecca is a long way from reintegrating her faith with her experience. Over many months she has explored pathways for healing and dialogue in a relationship that was once very dear to her. Roadblocks continue to arise, and Rebecca's efforts toward transformation seem to be foiled by an intractable gulf between her own needs and those of her former friend. As hard as it is for me to acknowledge that Rebecca's road toward healing is slow and difficult, it is crucial that I realize this and respect the process and the pace of change that she can manage.

+ + +

To love the dechurched is to guard against placing oneself as a spiritual authority over them. Such authority may have been abused in their prior experiences with Christians. A heavy hand will certainly be rejected.

Mary Anne attended a workshop I led about the world of the dechurched. After the event concluded, she stopped to talk with me. A sophisticated, well-educated woman with a doctoral degree in Christian Education, Mary Anne reflected on her relationship with a sister.

"I come from a family of four girls," Mary Anne commented. "As adults, all but one of us are actively involved in the church and deeply committed to our faith. My sister Irene has a son but never goes to church herself or takes her child to church. For years, the rest of us have bugged Irene about going to church. We have tried to coax her. We have tried to help her see how valuable it would be for her son. But it never occurred to me until now that she might have reasons for not attending church or wounds that block her from reconnecting to the faith in which she was raised."

Mary Anne needed to step back and develop new insight about accepting her sister. So often Christians are too eager to inform, teach, or even condemn their loved ones who have left the church, when these family members really need to be welcomed and embraced just as they are.

+ + +

To accompany the dechurched requires great patience. It can be an extremely painful journey for the friend, pastor, neighbor, or family member who remains a person of faith. The challenges to one's own faith are endless. The dechurched will at times use a friend or mentor to "test" their thoughts about Christianity. A Christian may become the brunt of that person's anger at God, simply because he or she is present and willing to represent the faith that is being rejected. The dechurched may find pleasure in trying to shock Christians with their statements or their beliefs. The journey back to faith is complicated. It takes a great deal of perseverance and a deep commitment of time and energy to accompany the dechurched on the road toward wholeness.

As difficult as it may be, it is critical to nurture relationships—whether with family members, coworkers, or neighbors—without a host of expectations that our helpfulness or spiritual insight will make a radical difference in their lives. Our input may be instrumental in facilitating change, or it may not. Transformation will not come from us. The fruit born through the relationship is nourished by God.

+ + +

One of my greatest struggles as a pastor ministering among the dechurched is dealing with the way the Bible has often been used as a weapon in their lives. Many defectors from the faith have experienced the Bible as a sourcebook of condemnation and shame. Instead of helping them to tell the truth about themselves and their lives, the Bible has been used to keep them silent. In short, the Bible has functioned as a vehicle of oppression rather than as an instrument of liberation and healing.

Barbara, a woman in her sixties, shared memories of her upbringing with me. She was one of five children. Her parents remained married to one another until they died well into their nineties. Barbara's family of origin devoutly adhered to a very strong and strict faith.

Throughout decades of adulthood, three of Barbara's siblings remained dechurched. As they moved into their sixties and seventies, they still refused to talk about God. Another sister, Betty, was a faithful church member. She had left the denomination of her childhood and chosen a much different church environment for herself than that which she had once known.

Barbara herself claimed to be a Christian, but she tragically never moved beyond attempts to appease the punitive God she learned to fear in her childhood. In a rare moment of honesty and insight, Barbara confessed to me that she had never really felt close to God. I wondered if these were the same feelings Barbara harbored about her deceased parents. "I always hear people talk about how God speaks to them, but God never speaks to me," Barbara confided. "I guess maybe that's what it means to live by faith, but I wish my faith seemed more personal. Even though I pray to God a lot, it seems that God never reaches out to me."

Barbara finally began speaking about the operative scripture of the household in which she was reared. "Children, it is your Christian duty to obey your parents, for this is the right thing to do. 'Respect your father and mother' is the first commandment that has a promise added: 'so that all may go well with you, and you may live a long time in the land'" (Ephesians 6:1–3). Whenever Barbara, Betty, or her three other siblings attempted to speak for themselves or confront some of the difficulties they faced in family relationships, they would hear their father intone the booming and authoritative words of the Bible, "Children, obey your parents!" Along with this injunction came the four unspoken rules of the dysfunctional family: don't talk about yourself, don't think for yourself, don't feel what you are feeling, don't trust the people closest to you.

Decades later, this scripture still haunted the five adult children within this family system. The actual text continues, "Parents, do not treat your children in such a way as to make them angry. Instead, raise them with Christian discipline and instruction" (Ephesians 6:4). Barbara's parents felt that they were doing the best job they could in following the commands of the Bible. They never realized the impact their severity had on their children and their children's faith. The painful legacy of the past lived on into another generation.

+ + +

It is difficult for the companion of the dechurched to hear and acknowledge such experiences. To open oneself to such testimonies can be a great spiritual challenge to the hearer as well as the speaker. There have been many times when I have gone to the Bible for devotional reading and found myself reacting with the words, thoughts, feelings, and rage of the dechurched. I have had to read and reread a text ten times, each time asking God to help me see it with fresh, unwounded eyes, to explore it again from the perspective of faith, not abuse.

As a pastor among the dechurched, one of my core under-standings of the scriptures is this: the Bible can be used as an instrument of both liberation and oppression. This is not a statement about the truthfulness of scripture or its inspiration. It is merely a statement about the functioning of scripture within our finite, fallen, limited world. In the world in which we live, the Bible is often used as a marvelous instrument of liberation. That same Bible, used in other ways, functions to silence, stifle, and rob people of the very inheritance it proclaims in the name of Christ. This oppressive use of scripture does not embody the good news that Jesus proclaims.

For the Christian who loves the Bible and finds in its pages the strength and sustenance for life and faith, this is a very difficult reality to face. Acknowledging the constant tension between the Bible as liberator and the Bible as oppressor is enough to label us, at best, as pariahs and dissidents in the mainstream church, at worst as heretics. Further, this paradox about the use of the Bible is not one the church is eager to confront.

Contemporary critiques of the church from former insiders provide potent challenges for Christians ministering among the dechurched. Such critiques bear special significance because their messengers have at one time directly experienced faith and congregational life. Over the years, I have read diverse perspectives on women in ordained ministry, some extremely opposed to the presence of people such as myself in church leadership, others extremely supportive.

I have also sought to read books by post-Christian feminists. Some have been written by extremely angry women who rejected Christianity and embraced other faith perspectives outside of—and at times in opposition to—their former faith. I listen for their pain, their alienation, their vision, and their assessment of what they found lacking in their previous Christian experiences. I try to approach their writings as testimonies of the dechurched, works that are sometimes completed in the process of articulating their rejection of Christianity. I seek to learn what I can from the words and struggles of these women. I reexamine my own faith and the witness of the church in light of their powerful and disturbing critiques. I try to take what I learn from these women back to my own exploration of scripture and hold the concerns of this population close to my heart.

The critics of the church are haunting voices that join many other choruses of cynicism and disbelief that surround us. Their stories are sobering. Their influence over young minds is staggering. Paradoxically, they provide a prophetic challenge to the church. They call the church to wake up to the pain of its own defectors from the faith and be transformed in that hearing.

Sadly, it seems at times that the voices of the church would rather intone theories of biblical inspiration and defend these to the death than listen to one dechurched person, deeply injured by the misuse of scripture, as she shares her sordid, anguished autobiography. It is not possible for me to continue ministry among the dechurched without holding before me this horrible truth about "The Truth." The Bible is both the book of my faith and the book of my pain. I love it, and I wrestle with it. I embrace it, and I struggle with it. In the honesty of that journey, sometimes others—particularly the dechurched—can learn to do the same.

It doesn't take long to realize that working among the dechurched is slow, painstaking ministry accompanied by frequent setbacks. As much as I have wanted many to wind up as committed Christians attending The First Baptist Church of Oberlin, that happens more rarely than I would ever choose.

I have an embroidered wall hanging in my office given to me years ago by a church member. It says, "Who plants a seed beneath the sod and waits to see believes in God." This gift remains a wondrous reminder for me as I walk among the dechurched. The process of coming to grips with the deep issues of one's spirituality, the old wounds that fester and do not heal, the chronic questions and struggles about the meanings of various scriptures, as well as the inertia of staying in one place for many months or years is often a long-term challenge. While single moments of transformation may occur in the lives of the dechurched, frequently such experiences are part of a much larger tapestry of slow miracles, baby steps from week to week, month to month, or even as incrementally as year to year.

We are impatient with the dechurched. We long for miracles that are instantaneous and complete. We want the healing process in the lives of others to be neat and tidy, to leave behind no rough or unfinished edges. We want people to say yes or no, to follow Christ or reject him and to be utterly clear about which direction they choose. We expect the dechurched to eventually claim for themselves the theological certainty or surety of faith in God that some of us enjoy. We want them to grow to be like us and then get on with their lives.

Nothing could be further from reality when it comes to becoming a companion among the dechurched. The pathway is strewn with shades of gray where we long for black and white. The questions that people ask may be ones that we ourselves have never thoroughly considered. Because they belong to the realm of faith and trust, many of the deepest concerns of the dechurched cannot be rationally apprehended and easily put to rest. Ironically, faith and trust may be the two areas that most easily elude these individuals due to past experiences that have left them feeling hurt and betrayed. The journey of accompaniment is long and strewn with obstacles. The one who walks among the dechurched had better be prepared for this.

The wait for slow miracles may outlast our time of close involvement in the life of a friend or neighbor. That person may move away, choose to travel in different social circles, or even reject our friendship. After investing ourselves in a relationship with such a person, the feelings of disappointment and sometimes rejection that we experience must be acknowledged and processed. However, unanticipated setbacks should not daunt those who sense a calling to love and care about the dechurched. Christians can always pray for these loved ones, friends, and neighbors, regardless of what behaviors they exhibit on the outside. God has a way of touching lives that transcends what we ourselves can do.

+ + +

Lynn's closest friend in college was Maggie. The young women met during their first week at school. The following year, each of them made a commitment to Christ. After this point, their friendship deepened. Maggie and Lynn shared their lives together within the context of a close-knit student fellowship group, as neighbors on the same floor of a dorm, and as friends who faithfully supported each other in the joys and challenges of college life. Lynn had every expectation that she and Maggie would be friends forever. When they graduated and were geographically separated, Lynn was comforted to know that the relationship they had built was based on Christ and would endure the test of time and distance.

When Lynn moved several states away to attend graduate school, she felt extremely displaced and lonely. She wrote long letters to Maggie, but they were never answered. Finally, she called Maggie one day to see why she hadn't heard from her. Maggie stated rather matter-of-factly, "Oh, I'm just not much of a letter writer, I guess." Lynn felt very disappointed. She needed her friend during this time of transition, and Maggie just wasn't there for her.

After Lynn finished graduate school, she spent the summer in Maggie's hometown where Maggie was working. She was overjoyed at the possibility of reconnecting with this old friend. Finally, the two of them would be able to see each other regularly. She wrote Maggie and said, "I can't wait to see you!"

Little did Lynn know that Maggie was going through her own faith crisis. After graduating and leaving the closely bonded fellowship group, Maggie began questioning her own commitment to Christ. Ever since the two young women had become Christians, Maggie had always envied Lynn's spiritual vibrancy and strong faith. It seemed to Maggie that a lot of her own commitment to Christianity was tangled up in her friendship with Lynn and her enjoyment of the fellowship group they attended in college. While Maggie was trying to sort things out, she was also quietly drifting away from God. When Lynn finally moved to Maggie's hometown, Lynn was the last person Maggie wanted to see.

Maggie spurned Lynn's importunities to get together and rebuild the friendship that had been so important just two years before. Lynn was devastated. Finally, one day she summoned her courage and asked Maggie to meet with her to talk. As the two women shared, Lynn held back tears. Maggie was calm and unemotional. Finally, Maggie said, "Well, Lynn, I just think that when you leave a place, you leave the people. That's just how I feel." Lynn went back to her apartment and cried for hours.

Three months later Lynn moved but sent Maggie her address. She still hoped that the day would come when this valued friendship could be revived. Two more years passed. One day, Lynn got a letter from Maggie. "Guess what? I've returned to the Lord," Maggie declared with a triumphal sense of finality.

Lynn wished that all the heartache she had experienced during the past four years of her relationship with Maggie could be erased in this brief profession of recommitment to Christ. Lynn was happy for her friend, but she found another part of herself unable to respond. Too many disappointments remained lodged within her heart. Would Maggie be willing to truly reconcile her relationship with Lynn, or would she just want Lynn to forget the past four years and act as if they had never happened? Even if Maggie had returned to the Lord, would she take the time to respond if Lynn wrote to her? How could the two young women repair this friendship that had been repeatedly fractured?

These are issues that both the dechurched and their friends must often face if they are to move forward in the work of reconciliation and transformation. The rejection that Lynn experienced from Maggie was not simply imagined. Lynn's pain was authentic. The visceral challenges of loving those who have left the church and/or their faith exact their own price from friends and family members.

Lynn answered Maggie's letter, expressing her own happiness about Maggie's renewed commitment to Christ. Maggie sensed that Lynn was somehow emotionally holding back. She became angry with the measured response Lynn offered. Maggie felt that all should be instantly forgiven and forgotten. Lynn, however, was unable to trust Maggie again after so many rejections. The close relationship that the women had enjoyed during college had been repeatedly shattered since that time. It needed to be carefully rebuilt if it was ever to be genuinely restored.

Years later, Lynn and Maggie maintain sporadic contact—but usually only when Lynn initiates it. Maggie attends her own church regularly and follows her Lord. Lynn attends a very different type of church and faithfully serves Christ as well.

+ + +

My own prayers for the dechurched over the years have shifted from specific requests for particular changes to quiet, but deep prayers of relinquishment. The longer I have walked with God, the more aware I have become that I rarely possess the wisdom to know what it is that God chooses to do.

In my younger years, I often assumed the role of Director of Divine Activities in my prayer life. "Please do this, God, and soon;

or that, and tomorrow," was my mantra. I had most things carefully figured out regarding what God needed to do. I felt confident that I just had to remind God what needed to happen, and God would oblige.

As the years have passed, I have grown to understand the egocentricity of this kind of prayer life. While I truly sought to listen to God as I offered my detailed prayers, I regularly turned out to be mistaken on many of my opinions and much of the timing. Now, it seems better for me to lift people up to the Lord in prayer and pray for them deeply without inserting my personal agenda for their lives. I then entrust them fully into the hands of the Holy One.

As time passes, I may witness the slow miracles that are hard-won. In some circumstances, I am not privileged to be present for these changes. I am comforted in knowing that my prayers are never in vain, regardless of whether I witness their results or not. To pray and then watch for slow miracles in the lives of the dechurched allows those who accompany them to develop the fruits of endurance, patience, faithfulness, and love. This is a worthy journey for any Christian.

The ministry that I share with my husband is, in many respects, a transient ministry. College students regularly come and go in four- or five-year cycles, with only a minute percentage staying in Oberlin any longer. In twenty years of student ministry with over two hundred and fifty college students, only one has actually established permanent residency in Oberlin for a number of years. The non-student ministry has its core of regular members, but the rate of transience there has at times been even greater than that of the students.

Several years ago, I came to a point in my pastoral work where I found it increasingly difficult to open myself up to new relationships. Burgeoning friendships were abruptly cut short by moves. Mentoring relationships deepened, then college students graduated. As I met new people within the community, my heart said, "Don't reach out to these people. They will just leave." I knew that this could not be a healthy mindset for any pastor. I had to do something about the growing temptation to disengage emotionally from the very ministry I felt led to do.

One day I was wandering through an area bookstore run by a Catholic laywoman. She stocked the most interesting collection of resources I have ever seen in a Christian bookstore. One title met my eyes and nearly leapt off the shelf as if it belonged in my hands. The book, written by Joyce Rupp, was called *Praying our Goodbyes.* Within a few minutes, the book headed back home with me.

I spent four months working my way through *Praying our Goodbyes.* As I began reading it, I made a list of all the people who had come and gone through the church during my fourteen years there, first as a pastor's wife, then as a copastor. I copiously developed this list of people. I could remember the nonstudents down to children's names and faces. The congregation was mostly elderly when we came to Oberlin, so several members had passed away. These, too, were names I placed on my list. Many students' names were easy to recall, particularly those who continued to stay in touch long after graduation. I reviewed short biographies of Oberlin College graduates accompanying church bulletins on Graduation Sunday. I pored over our well-kept guest book from our first ten years in Oberlin.

The list of good-byes grew longer and longer. Finally, I felt it was nearly complete. Over two hundred and fifty typed names stared at me from two well-worn pieces of paper. The list spanned generations from newborn babies to widows in their nineties. Charismatics, Methodists, Episcopalians, Quakers, Baptists, Catholics, Presbyterians, Lutherans—even a couple who were formerly Amish and a student from the Salvation Army were on the list. Years of good-byes marched along in stark procession, name by name, face by face, memory by memory. No wonder I was having a hard time wanting to build new relationships.

I decided to take three names a day and pray my good-byes. Each day, during a time of prayer and solitude, I gathered up the next three names on the list. In silence, I remembered each person before the Lord. I recalled specific moments we shared together, whether around our dining room table, in a pastoral counseling session, amid a family or individual crisis, or as part of celebrating a momentous life transition. I was mindful of my own pain and pleasure within that relationship. Some names evoked joyful memories, others evoked sadness. Some good-byes were gentle and natural. Others were abrupt, difficult, and filled with awkwardness. As I concluded my daily period of remembering, I offered each person up to the

Lord. I committed my relationship to each individual into God's hands. I left in the prayer closet any unfinished business between myself and the person on the list. Day by day, week by week, month by month I prayed my good-byes.

At the same time, I slowly read through Joyce Rupp's book, participating in some of the rituals of healing and renewal included among its pages. Gradually, restoration came. Peace enveloped my heart as I was able to release the past and regain my ability to continue the work of seed planting before me.

To minister among the dechurched is to accept the fact that one's role may feel woefully incomplete. Yet we are not capable of peering into the hearts of others and seeing how it is that God uses our presence in their lives. We can only hope and trust that the seed we plant will sometimes fall on fertile soil. Ministry among the dechurched is a unique calling that is often marginalized within the church. "This man welcomes outcasts and even eats with them!" the Pharisees and teachers of the law complained about Jesus (Luke 15:2). They could not understand his choice of company nor could they imagine the genuine interest Jesus took in people that they believed had not proven their worthiness or dedication to God.

Christian friends keenly feel the intensity of the pain and alienation from Christianity that the dechurched experience on a daily basis. This makes the journey of accompaniment a continual challenge. Willa's story clearly illustrates this reality.

+ + +

Willa's spiritual history is marked by both diversity and confusion. The divorce of her parents when she was a child has, years later, left a major impact on her life. Willa's strident use of sarcasm belies her pain and cynicism. She attended Catholic schools most of her life, worshiped with her family in black Baptist churches, and encountered the tenets and practices of the Nation of Islam through male relatives. At times Willa ridicules the practices and institutions of Christianity; at other times she grasps for her familiar Christian roots.

Willa has no patience with the window dressings of Christianity that are evidenced in ritual without substance or in emotion without thought. She yearns for God at the same time that she insists on her personal autonomy. She has serious and valid questions about the history and practice of Christianity as she has witnessed it within her twenty-two years.

I attended a group discussion Willa led on the topic of Christianity and the institution of slavery. She read quotations from published slave narratives. She shared particular scriptures used by North American slaveholders to secure the obedience of their human property. She played a rap song by the contemporary group Arrested Development in which they decried emotionalism without substance and the lack of social vision found within many churches.

Willa's passion and biting criticism of her own faith tradition reminded me, once again, of the power of the words spoken by the dechurched. At times these individuals are our "prophets outside the gate." Their unlikely voices cry out, calling the church back to its moorings, to a life of truthfulness about itself and about the book of its faith, the Bible. If we are unable to face the harsh realities and questions of which the dechurched speak, we cannot begin to touch either their truth or their pain.

+ + +

To accompany the dechurched often means that the very people we love and welcome into our lives, ministry, and fellowship do not find themselves in the traditional theological places that make most churches comfortable. Oftentimes, the statements that the dechurched make are accurate reflections of what they are thinking or feeling, but are miles away from the carefully shaped orthodoxy that is familiar to many long-term Christians who have never left the church. Working with the dechurched can be untidy business for the churched.

I remember talking with my husband, Steve, one day about the challenges of trying to help the doubter and the cynic move toward genuine faith. We were facilitating a student group whose mission was to provide a safe space for anyone exploring issues of Christian faith. By definition, "anyone" included seekers, cynics, and committed Christians.

We quickly discovered that many of the committed Christians in attendance were profoundly disturbed by the struggles and ideas of the doubters, the cynics, and those in crisis—most of whom were college students between the ages of eighteen and twenty-two.

As the dechurched verbalized their questions of faith and their negative attitudes about Christianity, the churched were uncomfortable. Several strong Christians simply left the group in pursuit of fellowship with like-minded believers. Others stayed, but mostly with a fierce determination to provide a positive testimony of the faith to the seekers and cynics, not particularly to learn something from them as well.

How could this small group meet the needs of both the believer and the doubter? Was this possible? While Steve and I struggled with this question, we also asked ourselves where else the doubter could go to express her or his spiritual questions and struggles, if not to a place like this.

Many times I have had Christian students who felt certain in their faith say to me, "It doesn't do much for me to be in a group that is dealing mostly with disbelief, questioning, and doubt." These believers prefer time with those who, like themselves, are clear about their commitment to Christ. I completely understand their need. Tackling the poignant observations and insights of the dechurched confronts our own faith in challenging and disturbing ways. It can be exhausting. In the exclusive company of the dechurched, Christians cannot experience the depth of spiritual nourishment they generally require.

Those who choose to walk with the dechurched must regularly seek additional outlets of spiritual nurture for themselves in order to continue this work. Yet there must also be places where the lives of the churched and the dechurched can intersect in thoughtful and honest dialogue. It is good—and healthy—for everyone when such opportunities exist.

How does the companion of the dechurched hear stories of the abuse of scripture, listen to penetrating, often valid criticism of Christians and/or churches, and respond to probing spiritual questions without finding one's own faith sorely stretched? This is an ongoing question. To offer faithful support requires a deep and abiding faith in the unending welcome of God. It also means entering into God's profound lament for people who have been wounded in God's name. Our sorrow is not merely our own. It is rooted in God's pathos for those who have been sinned against, for those who have lost their faith at the hands of others.

It is a great temptation to get so caught up in the stories and needs of the dechurched that we cannot step back and wait on God. It is also possible to begin thinking that we, the churched, have most, perhaps all, of the answers that the dechurched need, when in fact to a great extent they must discover their own paths as they untangle their experiences. Thus, establishing appropriate personal boundaries in relationships with the dechurched is a critical aspect of guarding one's own heart.

During the first few years of working in ministry alongside my husband, I struggled a great deal with boundaries. The faith crises of others quickly felt as if they were my own. I spent an inordinate amount of time blaming myself for events beyond my control. While some self-doubt can be healthy, internalizing the crises around me did not further my ability to reach out to anyone. Instead, I often found myself depressed with another's depression, anxious with another's anxiety, or angry with another's rage. It took a great deal of personal growth on my part to alter these patterns and to establish healthy boundaries between my life and the lives of those around me. I had to learn how to care, listen, and respond without becoming entangled in another's journey, regardless of the angst it engendered in my soul.

+ + +

Mark became a Christian while in college. He eagerly studied the Bible and participated in Christian fellowship groups for a time. After two years of active commitment, Mark slid into a period of total atheism during which he abruptly removed himself from his many contacts with Christians. As Mark graduated from college, he continued this pattern of bouncing back and forth between a rigid Christian faith and a rabid atheism.

Years later, Mark stopped by to visit Steve and me. Steve had just unsuccessfully offered his study group "How Can I Believe Again?" and we began talking about this experience. We shared with Mark our concern for the dechurched and what we had learned from trying to offer this group. Mark replied, "I think I need a group like that."

I cannot help but believe that Mark's rapid shifts from fundamentalism to atheism, which became established cycles in his life, had something to do with issues much more basic to his personal story than even faith or disbelief. Was Mark struggling with undiagnosed mental illness that created periods of instability and impacted all other aspects of his life, including his faith? Had there been some early trauma that Mark was not acknowledging? Did his moments of faith serve as a crutch to avoid dealing with some secret addictive or compulsive pattern of behavior? I do not know the answer to these questions, but these are all issues that would warrant significant exploration in Mark's life, should he ever really want to do the hard work implied in "believing again."

If I were counseling Mark, I would try to help him examine his patterns of faith and disbelief over the years. To simply help him recommit his life to Christ once more would be woefully inadequate. Mark needs to discover a faith that can endure, a faith that can speak to his periods of both belief and disbelief. Mark must uncover the roots of behaviors that have plagued him for at least a decade. By tackling this kind of inner work, I think Mark might eventually be able to truly believe again.

Any faith Mark might discover would surely differ from his past forays into Christian life and practice. Its substance and meaning would take Mark a lot more time to discover than the spurts of commitment to which he has become accustomed. Yet its cultivation would be well worth the effort.

+ + +

The companion of the dechurched must continually remind him- or herself that we do not have the power to change lives. This is the work of God. We can inspire, encourage, challenge, and embrace. We can ask probing questions when it is appropriate to do so. We can share our own stories of transformation. We can listen. We can love. But we cannot change another person. As we come to grips with this reality, we are freed from grandiose expectations of the value of our own ministries and how much we can accomplish as we walk alongside our neighbors. Ministry among the dechurched leads us into deeper and deeper relinquishment, not into collecting a list of success stories. When such testimonies do arise, they are the work of God and not of ourselves. The one who walks among the dechurched will be transformed by this ministry. Indeed, it is difficult, but it is not without opportunities for personal growth.

One day Amina brought a list of questions to a meeting with me. After facing a yearlong period of disbelief, she had begun reading the Bible again. A young Christian who had once embraced her faith with few doubts, Amina witnessed a vicious verbal attack on another student, instigated by a group of Christians. She was shocked by the lack of Christian charity exhibited and began to question the validity of Christianity itself.

For months Amina considered herself an agnostic. We often talked together about issues of faith and doubt. Amina sought to process her reactions to the incident she had witnessed. A year later, she cautiously began embracing her longing for God once again.

This particular day as we talked, Amina was wrestling with the idea of Jesus' being both divine and human. Indeed, this concept is not easily apprehended by the rational mind. Amina looked at a list of questions she had written on a tiny piece of paper and asked me, "Do you think that God ever regretted sending Jesus to die for us?"

What a question! In twenty years of ministry, I had never pondered that thought. Here was this young woman, barely nineteen years old, struggling with this idea as she wrestled with the possibility of believing again.

+ + +

I have learned a lot from the dechurched. In many respects, they have been my teachers. They have exposed the many ways the Bible has been misused to hurt and oppress people. They have allowed me to share in their experiences of great pain and unspeakable disappointment. They have helped me grasp a glimpse of human nature that I might not have gained without their help. They have forced me to question some of my long-held assumptions, grow in my own patterns of self-care, and nurture my own sense of personhood.

The companions of the dechurched receive as much as they give. I never tire of hearing the stories of this population. Yes, the content of their testimonies tears me apart. There are times when the pain and heartache they experience seem too great for any human being to bear.

I consider it a privilege to hear the stories of the dechurched, to be trusted with some of the most difficult confessions a person could ever make. I find deep satisfaction in being invited into the broken and restless lives of those looking for the pathway "home." I don't expect to be a rescuer or a savior. I expect to be a companion, a friend and fellow pilgrim along the way. I might be a seed planter. I might be a waterer. I might even get to witness the full flowering of the fruit on the vine. My journey echoes that which the apostle Paul describes in 1 Corinthians 3:5–9 (NRSV):

> What then is Apollos? What is Paul? Servants through whom you came to believe, as the Lord assigned to each. I planted, Apollos watered, but God gave the growth. So neither the one who plants nor the one who waters is anything, but only God who gives the growth. The one who plants and the one who waters have a common purpose, and each will receive wages according to the labor of each. For we are God's servants, working together; you are God's field, God's building.

CHAPTER 18

In Their Own Words: Testimonies of the Dechurched

Whenever I speak about the dechurched, the reaction I receive is immediate and intense. Parents confess their anxieties about adult children who rejected the faith of their youth long ago. Married Christians recount the struggles of living with spouses who no longer want anything to do with the church. Neighbors recall friends or coworkers who were once active in local congregations and no longer participate. Pastors name former parishioners, each with a unique story and particular set of circumstances. Ministry among this population confronts us everywhere we go.

As I began writing this book, I was acutely aware of the fact that my own experiences with the dechurched have been shaped within a specific geographical location and context for ministry. Many other factors that I may not even recognize or understand undoubtedly impact what I can offer as an introduction to the world of the dechurched.

With these realities in mind, I composed a questionnaire for the dechurched and formerly dechurched. I disseminated it as widely as my personal networks allowed. I advertised the survey in the

First Baptist newsletter, which reaches about seventy-five homes locally as well as 150 others around the country. Together, the newsletter readers represent a wide variety of denominational backgrounds and current church affiliations. Since many active members of First Baptist Church have been dechurched at some period of their lives, I encouraged individuals in our congregation to share their journeys with me through the survey questions as well. Several people near and far requested copies of the questionnaire for spouses, friends, coworkers, or acquaintances. About fifty surveys were disseminated.

I sought to ask questions that could help the dechurched recount their experiences of disillusionment and disbelief, of shattered and sometimes rebuilt faith. Knowing well the varied reactions they might have to reflecting on their Christian experiences, I realized that many would never look at the surveys. These had ceased caring about such issues long ago. Some would briefly glance at it and decide, *I'm just not ready to think about these questions.* They, too, would not take the time to document their responses.

Still others would wrestle with the issues presented in the survey only to harbor grave misgivings about sharing their responses with me. One friend I contacted said, "I have been working through the survey, and there is just too much rage in my answers. I don't think I want to share these thoughts with anyone, even with you."

Finally, a few would actively engage the questions on the survey, record their testimonies—perhaps in great detail—and then take the risk of returning their responses to me. They would represent only a small percentage of those who initially received the survey.

The vast majority of those who returned their surveys were formerly dechurched individuals already far along on the road of reconstructing their faith or engaging once again within a community of believers. This fact in itself highlights the challenge that exists in attempting to reach out to the dechurched. Many have no desire to reopen old wounds and simply prefer to be left alone.

I asked respondents whether they would be willing to have their stories included in this book. I originally hoped to weave their stories into the body of the book, thus amplifying the number of illustrations available to me. I also wanted to test my theories and conclusions against the actual reflections and observations of the dechurched or formerly dechurched. I was heartened to find that all those who returned their surveys welcomed a wider audience for their insights.

As I read through the survey responses several times, I was profoundly moved by the power of these personal testimonies. I was convinced that they would offer the greatest impact if they were allowed to speak for themselves. For the sake of length, I omitted minor sections, yet none of these omissions sacrificed the critical insight of the writer. I left the majority of their comments unedited, excepting minor grammatical changes or clarifications in wording. Most of the testimonies I received are included in this chapter.

It is only when we are truly willing to hear the stories and testimonies of the dechurched and formerly dechurched that these voices will begin to break through our defenses, challenge our methods of pastoral care, and confront our inconsistencies as people of faith. It is only when we are willing to wrestle with the cries of outsiders who were once insiders that we will begin to reclaim the true vocation of the church as the body of Christ on earth today.

The Dechurched Survey
A Sample of Responses

I am writing a book about the dechurched. It attempts to address the issues and concerns of those who have left the church and/or their Christian faith, as well as those who left for a period of months or years and returned. I am looking for true stories both to help me think through my conclusions after years of working with the dechurched and to offer additional illustrations for the book itself.

If you prefer, please feel free to write an autobiographical account of your experiences with the church/Christian faith and your feelings about being dechurched on separate paper. Otherwise, please respond to the questions listed below:

1. Describe your spiritual history, including your religious upbringing or experiences with Christianity as a child, what this meant to you, the struggles you had with your beliefs, etc.
2. When, and how, did you leave this history behind? How old were you? Was there a precipitating crisis? If so, please explain.

3. What beliefs and understandings did (do) you hold about God while you were (are) dechurched? Have these viewpoints been challenged at any point? If so, how?
4. For how many months or years have you been away from the church/Christian faith?
5. How much did you interact with other Christians while dechurched? What were your feelings about church, Christians, and Christianity at the time? What were your fears about God?
6. If you are not presently dechurched, what led you back to Christian faith and/or the church? Was there a precipitating incident or event of some significance in the process? How did your understandings about God, faith, the church, and Christians change?
7. Where are you now in your faith journey?
8. At your time of deepest crisis, can you think of anything that the church/Christians could have done or been for you that would have helped you navigate your faith or stay in your church community rather than leave these behind?
9. What advice can you give to the church/Christians who want to reach out to the dechurched?
10. Would you permit your responses to be included in a book about the dechurched?
11. If you answered "yes," would you prefer to have your first name used or a fictitious name?

A mother and freelance writer speaks:

My earliest images of God were: a big old man in the sky with white hair and a beard who, when angry, could make bad things happen to me (including death during the night, followed by the taking of my soul!). This could explain my childhood fear of Santa Claus.

I have no memories of any of my Sunday school teachers. I do recall being interested in the picture of Jesus hanging in the church. He seemed like a kind sort, and he knew some magic tricks (the loaves and the fishes, for one). I had no idea where he fit with this omnipotent, male, air-traffic-controller God (who, like Santa, knew if I'd been naughty or nice).

I spent a lot of my childhood being nervous and anxious, and I don't recall feeling any better or more comfortable in church. I had the sense that we were outsiders—we had moved from another town, we had less money than other families, I had been baptized when I was older than the rest of the kids, and my clothes came from discount stores.

As I approached adolescence (and the 1960s), I began to read more and more, and to ask questions more and more. No one seemed pleased about this. I was told that I thought too much.

On the day that Bobby Kennedy was shot, I stopped at "my" church on the way home from school. I wanted to pray. The custodian told me that the sanctuary was locked during the week. I argued. He sent me to the minister, who had recently "confirmed" me after I stood, sweaty and terrified, in front of the metal sculptures of the apostles and tried to remember the words I had so unsuccessfully memorized (I still can't memorize, but I can read with expression). This minister seemed to think that I wanted to steal something (what?) from the sanctuary, and he sent me home.

Soon after this (I was about sixteen, I think), I began reading about communism, etc., and I decided that there was, in fact, no God. When the church sent me a pledge request, I sent it back with a blunt note explaining why I was leaving the church. My parents were so embarrassed they never went back. I never heard from the church.

I wandered in the metaphorical desert for many years. During this time I focused on getting my education and starting my career. I also married and began a family. When my daughter was born and I decided to stay at home, I began to have more time to read for pleasure. I found myself thinking more about spiritual things. Something was missing from my life (and my child's). I tried going to a Unity church, but it seemed too much like a twelve-step church with a charismatic leader. When my family moved, I began attending a church where I found a youth program for my daughter and a group of people with whom I felt comfortable. There was a social action focus and an intellectual tone that appealed to me. There was also an unquestioning acceptance of people that I had not experienced before in a church.

A few months after I started attending this church, I was asked to join the adult education committee. The person who called me indicated that this invitation was based on the perception that this was something I would be interested in and good at. I was deeply touched, because women were usually asked to be on the social committee, not the adult education committee. It was important to me that someone had recognized my talents and acted upon that awareness.

The friends I made at church (including the pastor and his wife) were essential to my handling of my dad's death. Food, cards, notes, but mostly their presence helped me. My dad, knowing that my mom would be uncomfortable and sensing that I had entered a new phase, asked me to bring my Bible and read to him during his last days. He told me that he had talked to God and was not afraid to die. That changed my life forever.

My recent church attendance has been poor, but I know that I will never "leave" the church again. It will always be part of my life, in some form. Sunday morning services have never become a true part of my routine, but spirituality infuses everything for me. I read the Bible every day, a frustrating but essential discipline for me—I have years of catching up to do. I believe that where we perceive chaos, there is in fact order. I believe that we are here to learn, and that process does not end when we "die." I believe that what is ahead cannot be comprehended by us except in glimpses. As an adult, I'm better able to see the church as an institution full of people, never perfect, but with something to offer and as something to which I can contribute.

A young nurse's aide speaks:

As a young child, I remember going to church as well as Sunday school every week with my parents. We went to a Lutheran church. On holidays—Christmas Eve and Easter Sunday—Mom and Dad always brought me to the Baptist church to be with my grandma. Looking back, if I were to just look at the "picture" of my family, I'd probably say we were an average Christian family—because we went to church. However, if I look closer, underneath the "outer layer," we were far from being a Christian family by any means. Mom and Dad never talked to me about God, or church. When I asked questions, as innocent children do, the answer was always the same: "Ask your Sunday school teacher," or "Because that's just how things are, that's why." As one might figure, I stopped asking questions. The one childhood belief that I can vividly remember about God is when I thought God was "a big guy who I couldn't see, but who was able to take all my problems away."

Right before I started fifth grade, my family moved. After we moved, for no apparent reason, we stopped going to church on Sundays. No explanation was given; we just stopped going, except for the holidays when we would go to church with Grandma. I believe this is the first time I "left" the church. At some point, Grandma got me back into church. Dad would drive me to her church, but Mom and Dad would never come with me.

At the end of my eighth-grade year, though I didn't completely stop going to church, I held back and numbed myself spiritually. During this time I remember thinking, *God isn't for me. He doesn't care about me—why should I care about Him?*

I was angry that my grandfather was sick. I knew he was dying and I desperately wanted to make some sort of peace with him—I never did. I was angry that Mom and Grandma had signed a form that enabled staff to avoid reviving him if his heart stopped. I was very confused with the idea of just letting him die. Mom and Dad never really explained this to me—but by this time, I had already learned that it did no good to ask questions, so I kept silent.

A month later, my beloved cocker spaniel died in my arms. This event is what I believe made me run away from God. I became furious at God, as well as myself. During this time I went to church, yet I was very uninvolved. Everything that I heard from church—or other Christians—I either ignored or brushed off by telling myself that it didn't pertain to me.

My main problem during these times was that I didn't understand. I had so many questions, to the point of feeling overwhelmed. At some level, I think I really believed that God was "supposed" to take all my problems away and answer all my questions on the spot. When that didn't happen, I decided that the only "true" explanation was that there simply was no God. God, for me, was like Santa or the Easter Bunny. Over time, the overwhelming sense of needing to understand everything about God has been challenged again and again. At some point, I came to the realization that it is impossible to understand God completely. Although I still struggle with this, I'm no longer completely overwhelmed.

The second time I was dechurched I continued going to church and interacting with other Christians, but I withdrew emotionally and spiritually. I thought anything to do with church, God, or faith was bogus. It was just one big joke. I think, at this point, my biggest fear (though now I know it was completely irrational) was that God really didn't care about me, or if God did care, I was beyond forgiveness.

Coming back to God and my Christian faith was a very slow process. My views about God and faith started to change shortly after I was involved in a serious car accident. I realized that I could have died. This made me question my inability to know God's love. Through that questioning, I discovered some real truths about God's love, as well as a real comfort—one I'd never known before—through reading God's word. Through daily devotions, prayer, and reading the Bible, I have been able to reexamine not only my life, but my views and understandings of God, faith, the church, and Christians.

My faith has undergone some major changes. I used to have a faith that blew in the wind. If things went my way, I was "close" to God. However, if things weren't going my way, well—I ignored God. I know now that just because I believe that Jesus died on the cross for my sins, my everyday life isn't going to be perfect. Going through trials and temptations is natural, even inevitable. I know now, from experience, that one can either dwell on the "down" times and blame God, or one can use those times to draw nearer to God and build on one's faith.

Looking back at all these periods of my life, the church and fellows Christians tried to help me. I know now that people were trying to help me make some kind of sense out of what was happening in my life, but I ignored them and walked away. My advice to those who want to reach out to the dechurched is this: Be patient. Sometimes, as much as the dechurched want—perhaps even need—the church's help, if the church tries to reach out, the dechurched push that help further away. Be patient. Let the dechurched know you are there for them if they need a listening ear, but don't push them to talk—it just may drive them further from the place they really need to be.

A retired homemaker speaks:

My parents were Methodists. I was a country child who attended the Methodist church in town. I did not attend regularly, but felt enough of a sense of belonging to want to be baptized and join the church by the age of twelve. During my teens I attended church, occasionally inviting a friend to come along. When I married, it was in that Methodist church.

After I had children, my family attended various churches or church fellowships. I felt that I'd found the religious expression of my life when, in my thirties, I went to Quaker Meeting. I was the only one in my family to feel at home in Quaker Meeting for a long time. Our sons weren't interested and our daughters wanted to explore other ways of worship. Finally, when our children were teenagers, I felt the need to be in a church with people of many ages rather than a predominantly student meeting. Besides the Unitarian Fellowship I attended with my husband, I participated in a country church for several years. Each church was important in its own right and the right place for me and for my children to attend Sunday school for a while.

I left the country church and was dechurched again for a number of years. During my most alienated years, the world did not seem to have been designed right. I was angry with myself (which can't be a completely negative event) and angry with God who, being in charge of the universe, seemed to have invented a very imperfect creation (myself included).

I came to the Baptist church I presently attend through a talk by a missionary. I was invited to stay for services. I did, and I started coming with my husband.

Last year I was talking to someone about church. I used the phrase, "Church shatters you." I wondered about that terminology and decided that sometimes a church community can be transforming. In spite of differences in dogma and such, one can be accepting of the persons involved, and, being accepted in turn, break through the enclosure of self and find the self and be found in community.

I concluded that church helped me to accept and be thankful for the gift of other people; to struggle with the questions asked by my own life experiences when confronted by the questions and answers of a long biblical tradition as well as the responses of other people to their own life situations.

I believe there is that of God in every person, and that we are called to love God, to love ourselves, and to love one another.

There is nothing the church or Christians could have done or been for me when I left the church many times. I am convinced that my need to leave was a real need; it was part of my journey, my identity, myself.

A scenic artist speaks:

Like most PKs [preachers' kids], I went to church my whole life to age eighteen. I enjoyed church. I was baptized at age nine with a complete belief in becoming a Christian officially. Revivals at our church were very inspiring to me, and I always loved special musical performances. I was involved in the church youth group, sang in the choir, and baby-sat in the nursery. My close friends went to my church or other churches. The church was my extended family. My active youth group was an important part of my social life and certainly kept me out of trouble in high school. I had no real struggles with belief then. However, I did not agree with the guilt tactics and reinforcement of "original sin." I remember more than one youth retreat where sin was more of a focus than I cared for. Personally, I preferred to focus on the positive, and my father's preaching and leading was based on positive principles.

There was no crisis for me in leaving the church initially. It was merely a series of failed attempts at finding a church home. I also established friendships with people who were Christians and had gone to church through high school but no longer attended. These friends soon replaced my need for a church family. I finally settled, at age twenty-one, for working in a church nursery. I enjoyed being at church and having a church family without having to sit through a sermon every week.

When I moved east and stopped being a nanny, I tried several churches. I thought that once I settled into what felt like a permanent home, it was time for me to find a church home. I had a new partner in life, and this relationship felt like it was going to last forever. She did not grow up going to church and did not have a strong faith in God. But at first, she was willing to try some churches with me because it was important to me.

At the time in my life where I was open to finding a church family, a crisis did occur. In January of 1995, my mother wrote a New Year's letter where she expressed a concern that I was not going to church. She also said that she hoped I was happy. Then I wrote my whole family a letter explaining my problems with finding a church. A bigger part of the letter was trying to explain to them how I discovered I was a lesbian. More importantly, I said that I was happier than I had ever been, and I wanted them to accept my partner as a part of the family. I went on to explain that she had given up her country as well as her friends and family. Her father had terminal cancer and she needed family in the United States.

The letters I got from both of my brothers did not welcome my partner into the family. My younger brother was highly judgmental. He told me that I was a sinner and "must repent" and that God hated what I was doing. My older brother cited scripture. He was less harsh and more rational for feeling how he did. He knew people that had been "healed" from homosexuality, and I needed to join one of those groups or get counseling. My mother has tried, but it has not always been enough for me or my partner. At times my mother's response is disappointing for me, but she honestly tries, and she does not judge me. My father has never answered my letter at all. This stand of silence from him, and the persistent view of my religious, church-going brothers that I am a sinner have put a bad taste in my mouth at the idea of going to church.

I feel that organized religion is responsible for my father's silence and my brothers' insistence that I am a sinner. The whole episode with my family has turned my partner off from going to church altogether. After her father died, she would readily say that God didn't exist. The very people who brought me up as a Christian and my brothers who had the same upbringing cannot honestly say they accept my chosen life partner as a member of the family. And how can I defend Christianity to my partner when my Christian family cannot honestly say that who I am is OK? My problem with church-going now, at age thirty, is that people I expected to be supportive and understanding of my life have put religion between us and ahead of friendships and family expectations.

I have always had faith in God. I was taught from the time I could understand language that God existed and that he loved me. After finishing graduate school, there was a series of events in my life that reinforced my faith. Things fell into place for my personal life and my professional life. Jobs came just when I needed them and people helped me out. In spite of my feelings that a higher power was at work in making things happen, my partner challenged God's existence. She cited the usual views of "How can God let this or that happen?" noting the history of religiously inspired killings, pillagings, and taking of land. She also referred to the current trend of using religion to influence politics and social culture and thought that "religion is the root of all evil."

In undergraduate school, I had many friends who were Christian. As I went deeper into the world of theater, I met more and more PKs but fewer self-professed Christians. I do have discussions about religion at work with Christians and non-Christians. There is a consensus among dechurched Christians that churches are too political within themselves and that there are too many hypocritical people—people who say one thing in church and act differently in the parking lot and in the rest of their lives.

I currently have e-mail discussions with several dechurched PKs, and we swap information about other religions. I would not say that I have fears about God. I would say that I have doubts that Christ is the one and only savior of the world. Who am I to say that these other religions are simply wrong? Most have a supreme being, others have Christlike stories and teachings. Perhaps Christ came in different forms to different groups of people.

I have been dechurched for twelve years. I guess I am coasting, surfing the waves of faith and questions while waiting for some affirmation from my family members that may never come.

How could people have been helpful to me while I have been dechurched? My own family could have been supportive of my relationship. They used my own faith against me and extinguished my desire to find a church. I became completely uninterested in finding a church, even defiant. I suggested that if my father would respond to my original letter or at least write something welcoming and encouraging to my partner, I would be more interested in trying another church. My father was my spiritual guide for eighteen years. His silence is a hindrance to me. I have come to see organized religion as something that puts up walls between people. I have seen the good it can do, and now I am experiencing the bad.

It would also help for people not to judge. They could offer family-like support for life's troubles. Hearing "God has the answers" can prompt scoffing. Church and God can provide guidance in one's life. Church is a great place to help raise good kids. Churches should keep out of negative politics—attacking gays, abortion rights, etc. They should focus on positive politics—helping people have homes, child care, and especially basic things like learning to be good neighbors and controlling road rage. A Christian way of life is what I think needs to be projected. Faith and worship follow and then go hand in hand. People are unhappy in their work, in their relationships, and they look for answers and guidance. Christians can witness at work by being good people and not being afraid to admit they are Christian without being pushy about it. I feel I do that every day!

A mother speaks:

I grew up in an evangelical Quaker home. We usually went to church Wednesday nights and twice on Sundays. We were expected to be in church and participate in youth group. I treasure many things from my upbringing, such as the Bible knowledge I received. However, some teachings on women's place in the church troubled me greatly.

I faced a crisis over leaving my roots behind when my husband did not want to be part of the church we were attending. The church was advocating a dominant position for men and seemed extremely judgmental of anyone who would question their position on this and other issues. I can't say we were ever truly dechurched. We began searching for a new church home. We felt we needed to do this because of our young daughter. In many ways, God seemed more real to me during this time of searching. It was a period of freedom in my faith. Experiencing this transition reinforced my belief that God cannot be judged by who Christians are and what they do.

The force that kept me close to God and the church was my daughter. I want so much for her to have a faith that will help her cope with life. I also believe that God is much greater and more diverse than the God I was taught about as a child.

Perhaps if some compassion was evident and love shown in spite of disagreement on various issues, I would not have felt I had to leave the church I had been attending. Christians who want to reach out to the dechurched should not let preconceived notions and stereotypes get in the way of demonstrating unconditional love and acceptance. Caring for someone is not the same as condoning sin.

A retired teacher and social worker speaks:

I was baptized at a Congregational Church in Cleveland. I went with a neighboring family there. They were Frisian Dutch and were church-hunting then. My parents were not interested. They had been dechurched since World War I when they were young adults. My mother had plenty of religion at the Ohio Soldiers and Sailors Orphans Home in Xenia, Ohio. My father got out of the old Evangelical and Reformed Church. It was an immigrant church. My father and skeptical grandfather considered Christianity stuff and nonsense. My grandfather was a free thinker in the eighteenth- and nineteenth-century German tradition. But my grandmother believed, and the four kids went to church.

My involvement in the Congregational Church did not last because the Frisian Dutch family was persuaded to go to the First Christian Scientist Church nearby. They had a sister, "Aunt Annie," who was a strong-minded person who was also Christian Scientist. My parents never went, but I still remember the "Scientific Statement of Being." I had a text from Mary Baker Eddy.

This Christian Science experience lasted only about a year for me. I was then in junior high school. A friend of mine invited me to a Boy Scout troop at the Lutheran church. Their pastor looked disapprovingly at me because I went to the Christian Science church. I also was running around the church basement like the other kids were doing. It did not bother me much at the time. Some four or five years later my mother told the pastor off when he was canvassing the neighborhood. He said he simply could not accept Christian Science as a church membership or me as a Boy Scout. He got an earful from my mother.

Later when I was in high school my father and especially my mother went to a Lutheran church in Cleveland. My mother's heart disease and her weakness seemed to cause a change. Before that, my parents were mostly indifferent. I was drafted in April 1943, two months after my high school graduation.

After the war, I attended an adult Sunday school in downtown Cleveland. Mainly we were young adults from our neighborhood. It was really a social thing. The Sunday school teacher was quite concerned with my skepticism since I was a psychology major then and thought I knew everything about the human mind and its limits. This was before and just after I started college.

During my college years I occasionally went to church on Sundays, but not on a regular basis. I had political instruction in Marxism and dialectical materialism. I soon broke away from the Progressive Party. I knew Europe would starve to death unless we helped. The Stalinists were against the Marshall Plan. That was a time of political awakening. I did several restaurant sit-ins with the white and black students. We would time how long it took to get served, if at all, when a black person was with another white person. We used this information to expose racist restaurant owners in Athens, Ohio.

I was a psychology major with minors in philosophy, zoology, sociology, and German. I read some of the "higher criticism" of Adolf von Harnack. My mother, meanwhile, read her Bible. Both my parents still went to the Lutheran church. My father was not really interested, but my mother was mortally ill. Before my mother died she could not go to church, but the minister visited her weekly. No church members ever visited. Before my mother was too ill to attend, she visited the women's circle at the church. I remember her disappointment at being left alone during her last years.

The minister who visited my mother moved to another church. The new minister just back from the war was all right—but he did not make house calls—at least not at our house. My war experiences, college education, and my mother's being ignored by the church eroded my belief. I considered Christianity a superstition.

I married and attended various churches sporadically. I read a lot of current existentialist philosophy. I met other people during my dechurched years, but I was mainly in a college environment teaching German and social studies.

My fears were mainly for myself. I felt a void without meaning. Also, I wanted my children to have some connection with Christianity. I think the personal inner feelings of emptiness and the childrens' needs forced me to act. I read all of C. S. Lewis' apologetic, Jesuit texts, more existential philosophy, Karl Barth, and Reinhold Niebuhr. The death of my parents and my wife's parents contributed to my search. Today, I believe in Christ crucified and the coming kingdom. But I believe agape love covers everything. Brother Lawrence's book *The Practice of the Presence of God* describes where I am now.

Killing the Spirit and the Long Journey Home

The eighteenth chapter of Matthew's gospel provides the core text that calls me to ministry among the dechurched. This passage gives me hope as I listen to and love the lost and wounded ones in my midst. It provides perspective when I cry out, "How many, Lord? Must there be more? How can you bear all this abuse and tragedy, pain and alienation, perpetrated in your name?" Jesus speaks powerfully and poignantly through this passage:

> If anyone should cause one of these little ones to lose his faith in me, it would be better for that person to have a large millstone tied around his neck and be drowned in the deep sea. How terrible for the world that there are things that make people lose their faith! Such things will always happen—but how terrible for the one who causes them! If your hand or your foot makes you lose your faith, cut it off and throw it away! It is better for you to enter life without a hand or a foot than to keep both hands and both feet and be thrown into the eternal fire. And if your eye makes you

lose your faith, take it out and throw it away! It is better for you to enter life with only one eye than to keep both eyes and be thrown into the fire of hell. (Matthew 18:6–9)

There was a time in my life when I nearly ignored the text of Matthew 18:6–9. It frightened me. As I read it, I couldn't help but imagine the renowned artist Vincent Van Gogh cutting off his ear to appease insistent voices of insanity. The text's images of mutilation and drowning left me extremely uncomfortable.

As the years passed, I was drawn to this passage of scripture again and again as I ministered among the dechurched. Through sustained reflection on the teachings of Jesus and his ministry to the de-synagogued, I came to understand this text as a profound lament from the heart of God. This passage is in fact filled with pathos, agony, judgment, and hope. Rather than gloss over it, I now turn to Matthew 18:6–9 for strength and perspective when I can no longer bear the pain of the dechurched.

As I stop at the checkout line of the supermarket, my eyes often fall upon the latest tabloids. My senses are assaulted by inflammatory headlines such as "Two-headed Monster Found in the Ocean," or "Grisly Death in the Rockies." These newspapers sensationalize gruesome murders, psychotic rampages, shocking premonitions, and weird aberrations. I find their content disgusting. Yet the two metaphors that Jesus uses in the gospel of Matthew to illustrate the violence that occurs when a person loses his or her faith rival anything the tabloids can offer. These metaphors might make any Christian squeamish, particularly since they arise from the teachings of the Prince of Peace.

Jesus uses such violent metaphors to parallel a type of violence that is frequently silenced within religious communities—the violence of killing the spirit and losing one's faith. It is an ugly and awful act when it occurs. It is a murderous event in the eyes of God. Safe places to confess this tragic loss are few. Where can a person expose sexual abuse experienced years earlier at the hands of a professing believer and churchgoer? How can young adults untangle dysfunctional patterns of relationship that occurred in Christian families? Where can heartbreaking testimonies of Christian spirituality, interwoven and distorted by mental illness, be uttered and spoken? On and on the silenced confessions beg for release.

Matthew places this teaching of Jesus about losing faith between two very pastoral stories. In the opening of the chapter, Jesus welcomes a group of children after his disciples ask him, "Who is the greatest in the Kingdom of heaven?" (Matthew 18:1). The section closes with the parable of the lost sheep in which the faithful shepherd leaves the ninety-nine who safely graze in order to find the one sheep that is lost (Mathew 18:12–14).

The question that frames the entire discourse within Matthew 18 is the ageless query, "Who is the greatest?" This is a question of power, control, and dominance. It is a challenge by Jesus' disciples to discern the pecking order in the realm of God. The real question they are asking is, "Which *of us* is the greatest in the kingdom of heaven?"

Jesus provides a shocking answer for his followers. He places the most vulnerable, a child, in the midst of this group of adults. Children, who had no rights in first-century society and still have no rights throughout the world, illustrate to Jesus the meaning of greatness.

The story quickly shifts direction. Jesus grieves over the fact that such little ones can lose their faith. Children are weak, needy, and fragile. They can be despised and irreparably harmed. Jesus decries the potential within humanity to cause others to lose their faith. He paints a gruesome portrait of a victimizer's appropriate demise. It would be better for such an offender to drown in the deep sea, with a millstone cast around his or her neck, than to lead one child down the road from faith to disbelief.

The analogy Jesus draws is poignant and terrifying. The grisly image of a drowning person offered no avenue of escape arrests our attention. It haunts us. Yet Jesus uses this image to highlight something much more tragic—causing another to lose faith in him. Jesus makes a shocking comparison between the dastardly murder of the victimizer by drowning and the violent act of causing another to lose faith.

Killing the spirit is no small offense in the eyes of God.

Jesus is not speaking here about stabbings, muggings, or other outward acts of physical violence that are so commonly equated with sin. No, Jesus is talking to his own disciples, directly addressing their thirst for power, dominance, control, and greatness. His words of warning echo throughout the ages to the church that holds in its hands the power to both heal and harm, to testify to the greatness of God or become the enemy of the gospel of Jesus Christ.

Jesus acknowledges the fact that we do, indeed, live in a world where people cause others to lose their faith. "Such things will always happen," he concedes (Matthew 18:7b). Many who once believed no longer do. Many who once followed have left the path of Christian discipleship. This is a tragedy of tragedies that God endlessly laments. To kill the spirit of another deeply wounds the heart of God.

The impetus of Matthew's text quickly shifts to causing ourselves to lose faith. Once again, the metaphor Jesus uses is gory, almost psychotic, when viewed as a metaphor of self-mutilation. However, when understood in the context of amputation, Jesus' words offer an exhortation of hope.

> If your hand or your foot makes you lose your faith, cut it off and throw it away! It is better for you to enter life without a hand or a foot than to keep both hands and both feet and be thrown into the eternal fire. And if your eye makes you lose your faith, take it out and throw it away! It is better for you to enter life with only one eye than to keep both eyes and be thrown into the fire of hell. (Matthew 18:8–9)

When I was a little girl, my parents had a close friend named Al. Al had been confined to a wheelchair since World War II, when he lost a leg as a result of battle injuries. Gangrene could quickly have overtaken Al's body and killed him if his limb had not been severed. Amputation became for Al a life-saving medical practice that stemmed the tide of infection and ultimately saved his life.

In Matthew's gospel, Jesus encourages his followers to do amputative surgery on their own lives rather than run the risk of killing their own spirit. Figuratively, it is better to hack off part of one's body than to lose one's own faith. It is better to do radical surgery on our affections and commitments than to risk losing our love and devotion to God.

Many struggles of the spirit tempt us to lose our faith. Unhealthy relationships cut us off from God and replace our affection for the Holy One with dependence on human attention. Such relationships at times become spiritually, physically, emotionally, or sexually abusive.

They can stunt one's growth and compromise one's faith. Addictions also lead us away from following Christ. They can easily overtake a person's life and lead to a loss of family, friends, and employment. Materialism can cloud our priorities, driving us to choose financial security over integrity and faithfulness. A love for autonomy can delude us into thinking that we have no need for others in our lives. Anything that distances us from God, that drives us with a power of its own, can cause us to lose our faith.

In these two metaphors about losing faith, Jesus tells his disciples a great deal about their mission in the world. The violent images painted by the Prince of Peace bear haunting witness to the pathos of God. We hear the heart-cry of the Holy One who would prefer the destruction of a victimizer and the amputation of a believer's affections to the divine sorrow experienced in witnessing the loss of faith in even one human life.

There is no better conclusion for this text in Matthew's gospel than the parable of the lost sheep. All the gory imagery of the previous metaphors is banished. Instead, the scene becomes tender and inviting. The shepherd is compassionate and engaged. The sheep are gullible, dependent, and trusting, much like the child Jesus previously placed in the midst of his disciples. The sheep are prone to wander and cannot find their way home without the guidance of the shepherd.

The one sheep that is lost becomes the object of the shepherd's mission. The ninety-nine are safely herded, but the shepherd is not content until the lost one is reclaimed. Jesus reminds his followers that God does not easily let go. We serve a God who does not want any to perish. The Good Shepherd seeks the lost, one by one.

Jesus was profoundly grieved at the violence of losing faith. His sorrow was so great that he used some of the most graphic language found anywhere in the gospels in order to break the silence about this reality. This fact alone gives me strength to persist in my calling of welcoming the dechurched.

Christ is indeed the Wounded Lover, the determined Shepherd seeking the betrayed ones, the weak ones, the fragile ones, the despised ones who have lost their way. It is up to us to join him on this journey.

A Word to the Reader

It was painful for me to write this book and tell the many stories in its pages, but it would have been much more painful for me not to write this book at all. God gave me an enduring love for the church more than twenty-five years ago within a small Bible study group I attended at college. It is this love for the church that compels me to challenge the church to hear and attend to the cries of its own wounded. Paradoxically, the testimonies of the dechurched may provide a key to the ongoing transformation of the church into the image of Christ.

Much of the material I address continues to touch points of great conflict and even irreparable division within the contemporary church. I have not shied away from these issues. Instead, I have confronted them within the body of the text for all to read, ponder, and engage. I have sought to explore topics such as church structure, social relevancy, inclusivity, power, and prejudice as they impact those who see themselves as outsiders. I have examined the function of the scriptures, biblical interpretation, and our language about God from the viewpoint of the dechurched. I have tackled many of the "secrets" the church seeks to keep about abuse, trauma, mental illness, and addiction. To struggle with these issues highlights forgotten voices in our dialogue on the mission of the contemporary church. Such a discussion may also surface fresh questions to pose in the midst of the ongoing theological debates of our time.

I long for the day when the church is known within the world more for its honesty than its hallelujahs, more for its courage than its cacophony of voices, more for its sensitivities than its structures. I love the church, and I wrestle with it. I love the Lord, and I wrestle with my faith as well. In that visceral relationship between loving and wrestling, I find strength, hope, and life that cannot be extinguished.

It is my prayer that this book provoke thoughtful and vigorous conversation on issues too often minimized or ignored within our congregations and church structures. By the grace of God, may it be so.